VICTORIAN HOUSEHOLD HINTS

ELIZABETH DRURY

Copyright © 1981 by Harriet Bridgeman and Elizabeth Drury

1981 First published in Great Britain by
Adam and Charles Black Publishers, Ltd.
1994 Revised and reprinted by
PAST TIMES, Oxford, England

Printed and bound in Great Britain by
Biddles Ltd, Guildford and King's Lynn

Contents

ACKNOWLEDGEMENTS

In preparing this text I am indebted to the recollections of both servants and those whom they served. I am particularly grateful to Mr Arthur Inch for generously allowing me to read his unpublished reminiscences of a lifetime in service.

The poem My Nanny, written by Lady Diana Bridgeman when a child, is reproduced by kind permission of her son Sir Valentine Abdy. The illustrations are from The Lady, The Illustrated London News and Punch.

To Lilian Tyler, my Nanny

Household Servants and their Duties

In aristocratic households in the eighteenth and nineteenth centuries, servants learned their duties and skills from their superiors. Beginning in service as under housemaids, scullery maids, nursery maids, steward's room boys and under footmen, in their early or mid teens, they were taught their place and initiated into the daily routine of work by the servants who ranked immediately above them in the domestic hierarchy. They were supervised by the housekeeper and house steward or butler, who represented the mistress and master.

A large proportion of the population of Britain during these two centuries was employed in domestic service. It was likely, therefore, that young servants' parents would have been in service too, and thus were able to help their children in finding their first place. Some would have grown up on a country estate, making brief appearances in the house as children at parties given at Christmas-time and to celebrate the coming of age and marriage of the son and heir, their future employer.

Age, loyalty and hard work eventually brought promotion to the lowest of the lower servants, but, sometimes promotion could only be gained by transferring to another household. This required a good 'character', or reference, from an employer whom servants might barely know by sight and who knew them only as a name in the housekeeping accounts.

The structure of a household had not always been like this. During the Middle Ages, the upper echelons of the domestic hierarchy were drawn from among the local landowners and from the lesser branches of the master's family. The highest-ranking servants were of gentle, sometimes even of noble, birth: they were both attendants and companions. While attached to a household they acquired skills, and enjoyed privileges and preferment which would not otherwise have been available to them. In return they contributed prestige, armed allegiance and administrative strength to their master's household.

By the beginning of the eighteenth century the Medieval pattern of service had largely disappeared. Many of the original duties of gentlemen servants were combined in and devolved on a smaller number of attendants of humbler birth, who themselves required fewer personal servants. Some of their responsibilities were assigned to women, whose share and importance in the running of a house increased, particularly at the end of the century, when there was a growing tendency for gentlewomen to take less interest in the household arts and in their children's upbringing. In some establishments, the house steward remained, and he was often the only attendant of high birth. The Royal Household today is the last surviving example of a household supervised by persons of rank.

The composition of a Victorian household was rather different from that of the eighteenth century, although similar numbers of servants were employed. Women servants increased in number and importance, particularly in middle-class households, where parlour maids were often substituted for footmen. New kitchen equipment, the knife machine and carpet sweeper made some jobs easier and quicker, and household provisions that had formerly been made at home were manufactured commercially – but the same number of servants were needed to draw the curtains in the morning and evening, lay and light the fires and look after the family's clothes. Lunch and afternoon tea were introduced as additional meals, requiring extra preparation and organization.

In the late eighteenth and in the nineteenth centuries a succession of books appeared that were written to give advice to servants on the proper execution of their duties; others were intended to educate employers in matters of household management and in particular the handling of their servants. These books were for households where no traditions of domestic service existed: the households of the newly rich middle class. Chapters were devoted to the role of the Law in the hiring and discharging of servants, as the mistress of the house probably had to resort to the registry offices if her husband had no country estate and therefore no tenantry to draw on for servants of known background. Instructions were given on keeping a cellar book, answering the door in the correct manner, laying the table and waiting at dinner as well as on the tricky matters of precedence, modes of address in writing and speaking, and foreign words and phrases in common usage. These were questions about which no member of a long-established family or his servants would be in doubt.

The most comprehensive of these guides was *The Complete Servant*, published in 1825, and subtitled 'A Practical Guide to the Peculiar Duties and Business of all Descriptions of Servants, from the Housekeeper to the Servant of all-Work, and from the Land Steward to the Foot-boy; with useful receipts and tables'. The authors were Samuel and Sarah Adams. He had entered service as a footboy in 1770 and had been employed thereafter as groom, footman, valet, butler and house steward; she began as a maid of all work and served as housemaid, laundry maid, under cook, and lady's maid, progressing to housekeeper.

'A Lady of High Rank' wrote a dedication addressed to the heads of families for, claimed the authors, the book was as useful to masters and mistresses in arranging their establishments as to 'all Servants who desire to perform their duty with ability, and to rise in their career to higher and more profitable situations'. The general introduction addressed to servants included a long quotation from Dean Swift's sarcastic *Advice to Servants*: 'When you have done a fault, be always pert and insolent, and behave yourself as if you were the injured person; this will immediately put your master or lady off their mettle'; and again, 'When you stop to tattle with some crony servant, in the same street, leave your own street-door open, that you may get in without knocking when you come back; otherwise your mistress may know you are gone out, and you may be chidden.'

Positive instructions were given in Mrs Isabella Beeton's *The Book of Household Management*. Her domestic wisdom was first aired in monthly supplements to the *Englishwoman's Domestic Magazine* published by her husband, Sam Beeton, starting in 1859. In the Preface to the first bound edition, which appeared in 1861, she wrote: 'What moved me, in the first instance, to attempt a work like this, was the discomfort and suffering which I had seen brought upon men and women by household management.' Mrs Beeton began the book when she was twenty-one. Eight years later she died, but her book, a classic on the subject of household management and economy, has continued to appear in updated editions to the present day.

In *The Servants' Practical Guide, a Handbook of Duties and Rules*, published in 1880, it was observed that the manner in which servants performed their duties 'greatly influenced the smooth working of the domestic machinery, and that without the constant co-operation of well-trained servants, domestic machinery is completely thrown out of gear, and the best bred of hostesses placed at a disadvantage'.

The Adams, husband and wife, with their years of practical experience, Mrs Beeton and the author of *The Servants' Practical Guide*, based their descriptions of the duties and practices of servants in middle-class families on the example of servants in aristocratic families. They educated their readers in the ways of the British upper classes and so helped them to mix with their social superiors without discomfort.

The descriptions in this book of the roles of domestic servants are taken from these and other writings, and from the recollections of servants themselves. Their notions and wrinkles for polishing knives and shoes, cleaning decanters and ostrich feathers, packing china and glass, destroying bedbugs and pickling oysters will soon be forgotten as the days of footmen and laundry maids and packed servants' halls recede from memory. Some of the old-fashioned receipts, taught to each new generation of servants, are still useful; other are simply a record of domestic practices and standards of service in private families, and of a vanished way of life.

The Butler

In the great households of the Middle Ages, in which the duties of each man were clearly demarcated, the yeoman of the buttery, or butler, was in charge of brewing and serving the beer. By the beginning of the eighteenth century, he had taken on the work of the yeoman of the cellar, who looked after the wine, the yeoman of the pantry, who looked after the bread and salt, and the knives and other eating implements, and the yeoman of the ewery, who assisted the master to wash in the morning and at meals. By that date gentlemen who supervised the yeoman servants and their assistants had ceased to be retained as part of the household and had set up their own, lesser establishments. The server, who brought the food from the servery outside the kitchen to the hall, and the carver had both been gentlemen servants and the butler inherited their work, too.

Some of the chores involved in these new responsibilities the butler passed on to the footmen and valet, and he was their overseer. When the positions of chamberlain and house steward disappeared, the butler became the highest ranking male servant. In recognition of the fact that he had assumed the roles of the gentlemen servants, he was addressed as 'Mr' by the staff and his surname by the family; he hired and fired all male servants, except the valet, and paid some of the bills; with the housekeeper, he ruled the household, setting and maintaining standards of performance and behaviour among the servants. 'A Butler', wrote the author of *The Servants' Practical Guide* (1880), 'who knows his duties, and performs them with zeal, integrity, and ability, cannot be too highly prized by judicious heads of families'. Upon him depended not only his master's comfort but his reputation as a host.

The butler usually started in service as under footman, rising to first footman or under butler. Some employers would not consider a married man for the position on the grounds that 'the cares and expenses of a family probably militate against his being as well dressed and as smart-looking a servant as an unmarried man would presumably be' *(The Servants' Practical Guide)*. In the eighteenth and part of the nineteenth century he wore a dress suit, distinguished from that of his master by an old-fashioned appearance – perhaps because it was a cast-off of his master's – and some deliberate incorrectness such as the wrong tie for the coat or breeches when trousers were in fashion. In the latter part of the nineteenth century a black tail coat, black trousers, a starch-fronted white shirt, white waistcoat and tie became the butler's standard dress for the day and evening.

Widows often preferred to employ a married man, who was settled and unlikely to be the cause of trouble and jealousies among the staff, but, according to *The Servants' Practical Guide*, a further disadvantage of employing a man with a wife and family to support was that he might be tempted to commit acts of dishonesty: 'if the family of a butler were in great distress through the illness of his wife and children, or through other causes, having the charge of the family plate he might be tempted to raise money at a pawnbroker's upon any portion of article that was not in general use, or likely to be required before he was able to redeem it. This is by no means an imaginary temptation, but is one of frequent occurrence, as the police reports testify'.

The silver was in his charge and, by interpreting the hallmarks and the engraved inscriptions and coats of arms, the butler was often more knowledgeable than the master of the house as to the maker and date of a piece and the circumstances in which it was acquired by the family. When moving from one house to another, from the country to the town for the season, he selected and packed what was to accompany them, and from day to day scrutinized the lower servants as they cleaned and polished the table silver and centrepieces. Every night, before retiring, it was his responsibility to make sure the silver was safely put away. In some houses a footman would be required to sleep in or across the doorway of the pantry to ensure that the silver was not stolen during the night; or the butler's bedroom might be next to the pantry.

'The fitting up of the pantry must in a great measure be regulated by the style of the establishment, but, in any case, there should be a dresser furnished with drawers, one for table cloths, napkins and mats (unless all these be kept in side-board drawers); another for tea cloths, glass cloths, clean dusters, &c. &c. and another drawer lined with baize for the plate which is in use. Plate leathers, flannels and brushes, should be kept in a bag; and the cloths, and brushes used in cleaning furniture, in another bag to preserve them from dust' (Anne Cobbett, *The English Housekeeper*).

In some establishments there were separate rooms where the knives and plate were cleaned and the shoes polished. Trimming and filling oil lamps was a messy business and there was usually a special lamp room where this was done and where the lamps were kept during the day together with spare glass chimneys and shades.

A typical nineteenth-century butler's pantry was painted cream and brown, and around the walls were glass-fronted cupboards for the china and glass in daily use. The washing up was done in a wooden bowl with zinc bands round it, and there were wooden horses for drying the glass and tea cloths. In the middle of the room was a table and chairs or stools. There was a clock, looking-glass, notice board and plan of the dining-table on the walls, a butler's tray and a table for pressing clothes and ironing and folding the newspaper. It would have been surprising not to have found a picture of the reigning monarch and a few reference books, including a guide to the peerage. Hung up behind the door were the servants' aprons and on a shelf were a flat iron, a corkscrew, a funnel and fine cloth for decanting and straining the wine and a chamber candlestick for the butler to take down to the cellar.

'The keys of the wine and ale cellars are specially kept by him', wrote Samuel and Sarah Adams describing the butler's duties, 'and the management of the wine, the keeping of the stock book, and also of ale in stock, or in brewing, are in his particular charge. This duty he generally performs in the morning before he is drest to receive company, and he then brings out such wine as is wanted for the day's use. It is his duty to fine wine as it comes in the pipe, and to superintend the bottling, sealing it himself, and disposing it in binns so as to know its age and character.'

Ideally, the wine cellar was situated beneath the house, on the colder, northern side and as far as possible from the drains. To keep the temperature constant at 55° to 60°, a stove or chafing-dish was sometimes taken down there in the winter. Other articles required by the butler when the wine was not bought already bottled were a rope to lower the casks into the cellar, or a wooden plank or ladder to roll them down; a spade, birch broom and rake to lay and level the sawdust that some thought was desirable on the floor; various tools for drawing the bungs and corks, boring a hole in the casks and tightening the hoops round them; racking and bottling boots or cocks; wooden and copper funnels; a hammer or mallet; and flannel and linen bags for straining the lees.

Mustiness or acidity in old casks was remedied by burning brimstone candles in them or rinsing them out with brandy. Every butler had a method of detecting wine that had been adulterated by the tradesmen and of preventing the supposedly harmful effects of thunder. The Adams recommended laying a plate of iron on the wine vessels, while the author of *A New System of Practical Domestic Economy*, who was of the opinion that the damage was caused by 'a certain occult fermentation in the air', suggested lighting coal fires in the cellar to disperse the 'sulphureous and corrupting vapours'.

The butler's skills in the wine cellar ranged from knowing when to add ground oyster shells to the must to reduce acidity, to fining Madeira with three ounces of isinglass or Malmsey with the whites, yolks and shells of twenty eggs beaten together. Hartshorn shavings in cider and boiled rice mixed with alum and gum arabic were also used to clear wine. By following the Adams' instructions, he could convert white wine into red wine and *vice versa*.

The racking, doctoring and bottling of the wine was supposed to be done before the rest of the household was up and about. The butler tasted the wine before it was served and had plenty of opportunity to make sure that what was left did not go to waste. Insobriety, we learn from servants' manuals and newspaper reports, was a common failing among butlers and it was probably one of the reasons why, in the nineteenth century, the master of the house began to take a more serious interest in the contents of his cellar.

The butler selected the right wines for the food chosen by the mistress and her cook, if this were not done by the master, decanted the sherry, port and red wine, chilled the champagne and white wine and kept the cellar book. In the country he was generally expected to brew the beer; it was, after all, the original occupation of the yeoman of the buttery. Beer rarely made an appearance in the dining-room but was consumed in large quantities in the servants' hall and offered to tradesmen and visiting relatives. March and October were the months traditional for brewing, and it was usual to choose a week when the master and mistress were away from home. Water, softened by being left in the open air for several days, malt ground or bruised to a coarse meal and fresh, highly scented hops were required; a large copper, a mash-tub, an underback to receive the wort from the mash-tub, an oar or rudder for stirring up the malt, buckets, a strainer and casks.

Unskilled brewers might resort to fining their brew with isinglass or improving the taste with coarse oatmeal. Stale beer could be treated with mustard or by hanging a linen bag containing equal quantities of pulverised chalk and oyster shells inside the cask for a day and a night. The butler handed out the ale ration to the servants, keeping back some for those who were absent by reason of going about their master's or mistress's business. Where beer was not provided, servants were given beer money.

The making of cider (a cure for a fever and sore throats as well as a popular beverage in the West Country), perry and ginger beer was within the butler's province, and also sack, mead and shrub and liqueurs such as cherry, apricot and orange brandy. At Christmas-time he might mull the wine for the carol singers. Elderberry, cowslip, gooseberry and other English wines were generally made by the housekeeper.

The more servants that were kept, the fewer the chores that fell to the butler in the dining-room and pantry. His role in a large household was that of supervisor. Any criticism of the servants was directed to him; he was accountable for every wrinkle in the tablecloth or unaired napkin, and, of course, more serious problems such as the loss of a piece of the silver, found to be missing when he put the plate away at the end of the day.

Where one or more footmen were kept, the butler did not lay the table, but before the family was summoned he would cast an experienced and critical glance at the arrangement of the silver and glass on the table, making sure, for example, that the finger bowls – if they were laid at the beginning of the meal and not with the dessert – were exactly four inches from the edge of the table. For a dinner-party, he would choose the service and also the plate for the centre of the table and sideboard. 'In the management of the *plateau* and *epergne* he has many opportunities of displaying his taste, as these splendid articles usually consist of beautiful forms, ornamented with richly chased work, and designs of great classic beauty. It should be the butler's aim to place the stand to show those parts with advantage, which will contrast well with the highly polished glass and pendant lustre usually hung from the ceiling' *(Duties of the Butler)*.

At the beginning of dinner, according to *The Servants' Guide and Family Manual*, 'The order of taking up is the first dish by the Butler, and the remainder of the fish and soups by the Under Butler and Footman . . . The Cook is apprized of the serving of the soups and fish by the Butler ringing the dining-room bell; the removes or first course are then got ready; the soup and fish are conveyed out of the room by the Footman, who likewise brings up the next course which is placed upon the table with the same precision as were the soups and fish; the several dishes being placed on, and removed from off the table, by the Butler, and taken from him by the Footman.'

The meat was carved by the host and the fish of the previous course was divided by the lady of the house with the assistance of the gentleman next to her. When he was not at the sideboard serving the wine as the glasses were brought to him to be filled by the footmen, the butler positioned himself behind his master's chair and the first footman behind his mistress's.

During the course of the nineteenth century dinner *à la russe* came into fashion. Mrs Beeton described the new mode of dining in the first edition of *The Book of Household Management*. 'In some houses the table is laid out with plate and glass, and ornamented with flowers, the dessert only being placed on the table, the dinner itself being placed on the sideboard, and handed round in succession, in courses of soup, fish entrées, meat, game and sweets. This is not only elegant but economical, as fewer dishes are required, the symmetry of the table being made up with the ornaments and dessert. The various dishes are also handed round when hot; but it involves additional and superior attendance, as the wines are also handed round; and unless the servants are very active and intelligent, many blunders are likely to be made.'

The new way of serving dinner spared the cook from preparing a large variety of dishes – thereby reducing the cost – and, contrary to what Mrs Beeton maintained, it also meant that fewer servants were required to wait at table. According to *The Servants' Practical Guide*, 'In waiting at table the average attendance required is one servant to three persons; thus three servants are required to wait on nine people, and so on in proportion, an additional servant to every three additional guests; when a butler and one footman only are kept, extra servants are hired according to the number of guests invited . . . In the country this need is supplied by each guest or married couple bringing a footman with them, who, as a rule, is expected to wait at dinner, so that in some country house dinner-parties the attendance averages, perhaps, one servant to two persons'.

The butler, whose job it was to arrange for additional servants on special occasions, was warned that 'the traditional greengrocer from round the corner or a waiter from a confectioner's, are not the best class of waiters to employ for the purpose, or from whom good waiting is to be expected; servants out of place, personally known to the butler, or persons who have formerly been gentlemen's servants, are most to be depended upon.'

At the end of dinner the butler served the wine with the dessert and then, leaving full decanters on the table in front of the master of the house, withdrew with the other servants. He was summoned by a bell if more wine were wanted and, after the mid-nineteenth century, when the gentlemen, whom their ladies left alone to drink, were ready for coffee.

Until the mid-nineteenth century tea or coffee was prepared by the ladies when they retired from the dining-room after the dessert. Outside the hearing of the servants and the ladies, the gentlemen discussed politics and subjects of masculine interest until – some considerable time later, on many occasions, and more than satisfied with the wit and salacity of their own company and the generous beverages provided by the host – they joined the ladies for tea or coffee.

In the words of Mrs Beeton, 'Dining is the privilege of civilization. The rank which a people occupy in the grand scale may be measured by their way of taking their meals, as well as by their way of treating their women. The nation which knows how to dine has learnt the leading lesson of progress. It implies both the will and the skill to reduce to order, and surround with idealisms and graces, the more material conditions of human existence; and wherever that will and that skill exist, life cannot be wholly ignoble'. And however ironically we may regard these views today, Mrs Beeton's contemporaries were certainly very rigorous in maintaining high standards and paying scrupulous attention to detail.

Dinner, whether it took place at two o'clock, at half-past four or five, as it did in the late eighteenth century, or at the even later hour of eight from the mid-nineteenth century, was the most splendid meal of the day. It was the longest and was served with the greatest ceremony. Wax candles, which, because of their expense were regarded as a luxury, were used less sparingly than at other times and, even after the advent of gas and electric light and paraffin lamps, they were preferred because of the warm light that was reflected from the silver and glass and gilded porcelain on a well-furnished dining-table.

Breakfast was generally scheduled for half-past nine in the late eighteenth century, and it was on the table for latecomers until twelve. The usual role of the butler was to pour out tea and coffee at a side-table or assist the mistress by handing the cups filled by her on a salver. In some houses each person was handed his letters on a salver as he sat at table.

Luncheon was described in 1880 as 'an inconsequential meal', and in the Oxford English Dictionary as 'a slight repast taken between two meal-times'. When dinner was at half-past four or five and breakfast could be eaten at any time up until midday, it was not really necessary. The gentlemen were frequently absent from luncheon, engaged in some business or sporting activity, but it was sometimes attended by older children as the principal meal of their day.

From the mid-nineteenth century onwards dinner was served two or three hours later than previously, and five o'clock tea came into being as 'a light refreshment to break what would otherwise be a six hours' abstinence between two o'clock luncheon, and an eight o'clock dinner'. The tea was made by the housekeeper, or, if there were none, by the lady's maid or cook, and the butler usually assisted only if the number of people present were more than the footman or the parlourmaid could attend to single-handed.

At an evening entertainment, supper was served at midnight or one o'clock. In London the master of the house would dine at his club so that preparations could be made throughout the evening. Whereas the butler announced luncheon and dinner to the guests in the drawing-room, at supper he had to seek out the master and mistress from the assembled company to inform them that supper was served. A buffet supper was acceptable if space were limited, but it was customary to set up a large central table in the dining-room or billiards room and small tables for four or six around the edge of the room so that all the guests could be seated, though not at the same time. More than ever the butler had to be watchful. It was almost always necessary to hire servants, and even extra plate, for the evening.

At the beginning of the evening, the butler ushered the guests from the hall to the door of the ballroom or drawing-room. There, in a tone that would seem to be inviting a confidence, he asked 'What name, if you please, sir', waiting until the host and hostess had finished welcoming the previous guests before announcing their names in a contrastingly bold tone of voice.

The end of the evening is described in *The Servants' Practical Guide*: 'As the carriages are ordered at a certain hour, the servants of the guests are waiting in the hall at the exact hour at which carriages have been ordered, so as to be in readiness to call them up. The linkman on duty outside the door calls out the name of the owner of each carriage, which is repeated by the footman in the hall, that the guests may hear their carriages announced, and if they are not in readiness to leave at the moment a carriage is announced, it is sent on to make way for the next. When the guests are in readiness to leave, the butler, in answer to "Mrs. Blank's carriage," calls out "Mrs. Blank coming out".'

Paying calls was an important part of social life both among the aristocracy and middle classes. In answering the door to morning and, in the late nineteenth century, afternoon callers, it was necessary for the servants to know whether the mistress were 'at home', that is, whether she wished to receive visitors. She made known her intentions to the butler, who, in large establishments informed the footman on hall duty. In smaller establishments the butler might answer the door himself. Where only one footman was kept, it fell to the butler to open the door and attend to callers when the footman was out with the carriage.

If the lady of the house were 'at home' to callers, the visitor would be announced in the drawing-room by the butler, or shown into the drawing-room and asked to wait. If the lady of the house were not 'at home', the visitor would leave her card with the servant who answered the door.

There were visits of ceremony or courtesy, visits of friendship and visits of congratulation or condolence, and rules of etiquette applied to each: 'In making a first call, either upon a newly-married couple or persons newly arrived in the neighbourhood, a lady should leave her husband's card, together with her own, at the same time stating that the profession or business in which he is engaged has prevented him from having the pleasure of paying the visit with her. It is a custom with many ladies, when on the eve of an absence from neighbourhood, to leave or send their own and husband's cards, with the letters P.P.C. in the right-hand corner. These letters are the initials of the French words *Pour prendre congé*, meaning "To take leave," or P.D.A., *Pour dire adieu*, "To say goodbye" ' *(The Book of Household Management,* 1888). When calling to enquire after a person in ill health, it was usual to turn up the lower right-hand corner of the card. Callers on business were asked to wait in the hall while the butler took the card on a salver to his master or mistress.

In large and fashionable establishments the ushering and announcing of guests had originally been the responsibility of the groom of the chambers, who was also in charge of the appearance of the downstairs rooms, making certain that there were paper and ink on the writing-tables and keeping watch on the fires and lamps. In the course of time the butler assumed these duties, and by the nineteenth century he was paying the menservants in most households, and ordering and settling the accounts for the wine, spirits, malt and coals, which originally had been done by the house steward.

It was in the nineteenth century that the butler achieved his greatest influence and, with such power in his hands, there was a danger that he might become too proud for his own good. *The Servants' Practical Guide* offered cautionary advice to the butler who grew condescending: 'servants who consider themselves to be very high-class domestics, have a way of taking the management of affairs into their own hands, not always palatable to their mistresses, such management being invariably attended by a considerable increase in the household expenditure. They order things on their own responsibility; they change the tradespeople on the same principle. When a butler holding these views is at the head of an establishment, the mistress of it stands greatly in awe of him, and hardly ventures to invite a guest to dinner without giving him full notice of her intention.'

But there were butlers who shared the tips honestly, even generously, who taught the footmen and lower servants all the secrets of their trade and set them on the ladder of the domestic hierarchy by recommendation. They entertained them and the younger members of the family with stories of life in service; disciplined the boot boy and the heir to the family's fortunes and from time to time turned a blind eye to the activities of them both. They bore themselves with integrity and performed their duties zealously, which in turn imposed the highest standards on the other household servants.

The Butler's Instructions and Receipts

WINE POSSET

Boil some slices of white bread in a quart of milk; when soft, take it off the fire, grate in half a nutmeg, and a little sugar. Pour it out, put in a pint of sweet wine by degrees, and serve it with toasted bread.

The Housekeeper's Receipt Book, 1813

TO PREVENT STOPPERS STICKING

Wrap a piece of thin paper round each stopper before you put it away.

    If the stopper should at any time stick, breathe on it, or put one or two drops of sweet oil round the stopper, close to the mouth of the bottle, or just dip the neck of the decanter into warm *(not hot)* water, and it will soon loosen.

James Williams, *The Footman's Guide*

TO TRY THE GOODNESS OF SPIRITS

Set fire to some in a spoon; if good it will burn brightly away, without leaving any moisture in the spoon.

Samuel and Sarah Adams, *The Complete Servant*, 1825

CHERRY BRANDY

Stone six pounds of black cherries (guines); pour on them four quarts of the best brandy; bruise the stones in a mortar, and put the kernels in with the cherries; cover them close, and let the whole stand for a fortnight; then squeeze them clean from sediment, through muslin. Boil two pounds of very white sugar to clear syrup; mix it with the strained brandy, and bottle it into clear dry bottles. It may be used in two months, and should be kept in a cool cellar.

A New System of Practical Domestic Economy, 1824

TO MAKE GINGER BEER

Take an ounce of powdered ginger, half an ounce of cream of tartar, a large lemon sliced, two pounds of lump sugar, and one gallon of water; mix all together, and let it simmer over the fire for half an hour, then put a tablespoon of yeast to it, let it ferment a little time, and then put it into stone pint bottles, and cork it down closely for use.

Samuel and Sarah Adams, *The Complete Servant*, 1825

TO BOTTLE WINE

Having thoroughly washed and dried the bottles, supposing they have been before used for the same kind of wine, provide corks, which will be improved by being slightly boiled, or at least steeped in hot water, – a wooden hammer or mallet, a bottling-boot, and a squeezer for the corks. Bore a hole in the lower part of the cask with a gimlet, receiving the liquid stream which follows in the bottle and filterer, which is placed in a tub or basin. This operation is best performed by two persons, one to draw the wine, the other to cork the bottles. The drawer is to see that the bottles are up to the mark, but not too full, the bottle being placed in a clean tub to prevent waste. The corking-boot is buckled by a strap to the knee, the bottle placed in it, and the cork, after being squeezed in the press, driven in by a flat wooden mallet.

Mrs Isabella Beeton, *The Book of Household Management*, 1861

TO DECANT WINE

Be careful not to shake or disturb the crust when moving it about, or drawing the cork, particularly Port wine. Never decant wine without a wine-strainer, with some fine cambric in it, to prevent the crust, and bits of cork going into the decanter. In decanting Port wine do not drain it too near; there are generally two-thirds of a wine glass of thick dregs in each bottle, which ought not to be put in; but in white wine there is not much settling; pour it out however slowly, and raise the bottle up gradually; the wine should never be decanted in a hurry, therefore always do it before the family sit down to dinner. Do not jostle the decanters against each other when moving them about, as they easily break when full.

Samuel and Sarah Adams, *The Complete Servant*, 1825

FLIP

While a quart of ale is warming on the fire, beat 3 or 4 eggs with 4 oz. moist sugar, a teaspoonful of grated ginger or nutmeg, and a quart of good old rum or brandy. When the ale is near boiling, pour it into one pitcher, the eggs and rum into another, and turn it from one pitcher to the other, until smooth as cream.

Anne Cobbett, *The English Housekeeper*, 1842

TO MULL WINE

Boil the quantity you choose, of cinnamon, nutmeg grated, cloves or mace, in a 1/4 pint of water; add a pint of port, and sugar to taste, boil it up, and serve, with thin slices of toast.

Anne Cobbett, *The English Housekeeper*, 1842

TO MAKE WINE SETTLE WELL

Take a pint of wheat, and boil it in a quart of water, till it burst and become soft; then squeeze it through a linen cloth, and put a pint of the liquor into the hogshead of unsettled white wine; stir it well about, and it will become fine.

Samuel and Sarah Adams, *The Complete Servant*, 1825

THE POPE'S POSSET

Blanch, pound, then boil in a little water, $1/2$ lb. sweet, and a very few bitter almonds, strain, and put the liquid into a quart of heated white wine, with sugar to sweeten; beat well, and serve hot.

Anne Cobbett, *The English Housekeeper*, 1842

TO DETECT ADULTERATED WINE

Heat equal parts of oyster-shells and sulphur together, and keep them in a white heat for fifteen minutes, and when cold, mix them with an equal quantity of cream of tartar; put this mixture into a strong bottle with common water to boil for one hour, and then decant into ounce phials, and add 20 drops of muriatic acid to each; this liquor precipitates the least quantity of lead, copper, &c. from wines in a very sensible black precipitate.

Samuel and Sarah Adams, *The Complete Servant*, 1825

TO CLEAN DECANTERS

Cut some thick brown paper into very small bits, so as to go with ease into the decanter; shred a little soap very fine, and put it, together with some milk-warm water, into the decanters. The water must on no account be hot, or it will certainly split the glass. If the decanter be very dirty, add a little pearl-ash.

By the end of a piece of cane with a bit of sponge tied at one end, you will, by working this mixture about in the decanter, soon remove the crust or stain of the wine, and, by rinsing the glass once or twice with clean cold water, it will have a very fine polish.

When the decanters have been properly washed, turn them down in a rack to dry, or for want of a rack, into a jug, to drain thoroughly; for if not used for some time, and spots of damp have been left in them, a kind of mildew will be formed, which will injure the flavour of whatever is put therein, and prevent the decanter having that clear bright lustre which all clean glass should always possess.

James Williams, *The Footman's Guide*

ORANGE BRANDY *(Excellent)*

INGREDIENTS.– *To every ¹/₂ gallon of brandy allow ³/₄ pint of Seville orange-juice, 1¹/₄ lb. of loaf sugar.*

Mode.– To bring out the full flavour of the orange-peel, rub a few lumps of the sugar on 2 or 3 unpared oranges, and put these lumps to the rest. Mix the brandy with the orange-juice, strained, the rinds of 6 of the oranges pared very thin, and the sugar. Let all stand in a closely-covered jar for about 3 days, stirring it 3 or 4 times a day. When clear, it should be bottled and closely corked for a year; it will then be ready for use, but will keep any length of time. This is a most excellent stom-achic when taken pure in small quantities; or, as the strength of the brandy is very little deteriorated by the other ingredients, it may be diluted with water.

Time.– To be stirred every day for 3 days. *Average cost. 7s*

Sufficient to make 2 quarts. *Seasonable.*– Make this in March.

Mrs Isabella Beeton, *The Book of Household Management*, 1861

SACK

To every quart of water put a sprig of rue, and to every gallon a handful of fennel roots; boil half an hour, then strain, and to every gallon of the liquor 3 lb. of honey, boil two hours, and skim well. When cold, pour it into a clean cask; let it stand a year, then bottle it.

Anne Cobbett, *The English Housekeeper*, 1842

SHRUB

To 1 quart of strained orange juice, put 2 lb. loaf sugar, and 9 pints of rum or brandy; also the peels of half the oranges. Let it stand one night, then strain, pour into a cask, and shake it four times a day for four days. Let it stand till fine, then bottle it.

Anne Cobbett, *The English Housekeeper*, 1842

TO RENDER RED WINE WHITE

If a few quarts of well-skimmed milk be put to a hogshead of red wine, it will soon precipitate the greater part of the colour, and leave the whole nearly white; and this is of known use in the turning red wines, when pricked, into white; in which a small degree of acidity is not so much perceived.

Milk is, from this quality of discharging colour from wines, of use also to the wine-coopers, for the whitening of wines that have acquired a brown colour from the cask, or from having been hastily boiled before fermenting; for the addition of a little skimmed milk, in these cases, precipitates the brown colour, and leaves the wines almost limpid, or of what they call a water whiteness, which is much coveted abroad in wines as well as in brandies.

Samuel and Sarah Adams, *The Complete Servant*, 1825

TO MAKE PUNCH

Put *40 grains of citric acid,*
7 full drops of essence of lemon,
7 oz. of lump sugar,
in a quart mug; pour over 1 pint of boiling water, when the sugar is melted, stir; then add 1/2 pint of rum, and 1/4 pint of brandy.

Samuel and Sarah Adams, *The Complete Servant*, 1825

MEAD

Boil 32 lb. new honey in 13 gallons of water, and scum it well. Then add rosemary, thyme, bay-leaves, sweet brier, one handful altogether; boil it an hour, put it into a tub or pan, with 2 or 3 good handfuls of down ground malt; stir well till lukewarm, and strain it through a cloth into another tub; put in a round of toast, spread with yeast. When the liquor is covered with yeast, pour it into a cask, add 1 1/2 oz. each, of cloves, mace, and nutmeg, and 1 oz. ginger sliced, tied in a bag and hung in the cask. Stop close six months, then bottle it.

Anne Cobbett, *The English Housekeeper*, 1842

The Footman

The footman's domain was the pantry and the small rooms and cupboards where the plate, cutlery, china, glass and lamps were kept and prepared for use upstairs. At different times he was on duty in the dining-room, the drawing-room, the entrance hall, and outside on foot or with the carriage. His business, according to *The Complete Servant* was 'multifarious and incessant'.

Originally, footmen were outdoor servants, attendants who walked or ran beside their master's and mistress's horse or carriage. In the seventeenth century they were brought into the house to help wait at the lower tables. When the gentlemen and yeomen servants disappeared from all but royal establishments, footmen replaced them as waiters, at the master's table, supervised by a butler or under butler. They continued to perform some outdoor duties, and a footman whose particular job it was to deliver messages was known as a 'running footman'; but from that time they ranked as indoor servants.

When waiting at table, answering the door and announcing callers, accompanying master and mistress, carrying messages and undertaking commissions on their behalf, the footman wore his employer's livery. Of all the household servants he was the most splendidly attired.

Livery derived from the distinctive dress 'de-livered' by a Medieval sovereign or nobleman to his retainers. A servant was then his master's defender and there was no distinction between civilian and soldier. The scarlet and blue livery of the Royal Household dates from Queen Anne's reign; by that date, however, the business and dress of the civilian soldier had diverged, the soldier's dress becoming known as 'uniform'. The colours of most noblemen's liveries were determined by the colours of the wreath of two bands of silk on which their crests were borne – generally gold or silver and the principal colour of the coat of arms.

Because of the footman's original role, his livery resembled the coachman's in style. A large household would keep three distinct types of livery for the use of its footmen, each appropriate to different occasions. State livery, worn only on state occasions, differed little from the full dress livery, except in the degree of elaboration of the trimmings. Both liveries were ornamented with the footman's 'trademark', the aiguillette, an article of gentlemen's dress in the late seventeenth century. Known also as the shoulder knot, it gave its name to the footman's informal title 'Knight of the Shoulder Knot'. It consisted of ribbon, braid or cord loops terminating in metal tags, or aiglets, worn from the right shoulder, though 'When two footmen attend the carriage, it is permissible for the head footman's aiguillette to proceed from the right shoulder and the second footman's from the left. This plan has a good effect, and prevents the one's aiguillette from rubbing against the shoulder of the other man' *(The West-End Hand Book of British Liveries)*. Another symbol of office was the cane with a gold or silver knob carried out of doors by many nineteenth-century footmen.

A distinctive detail of the footman's undress livery, the third type, was the waistcoat of striped valencia. Indoor servants wore waistcoats with horizontal stripes while the stripes were vertical for outdoor servants, except in the Royal Household, where all the menservants, whatever their occupation, wore waistcoats with vertical stripes. Waistcoats worn with state and full dress livery were generally white or the same colour as the coat.

The most sumptuous article of the footman's livery was his full dress coat. The cut was that of the coat 'worn by all classes of persons above the grade of labourer in the reign of George I'. It had gold or silver buttons stamped with the family's crest or the initial of his master's or mistress's surname, collar and cuffs generally of a contrasting colour, shoulder knot, épaulettes and elaborate trimmings.

Although footmen had been forbidden by the Earl Marshal in 1701 'to wear swords, or any offensive weapon, within the cities of London and Westminster, and the liberties and precincts of the same', a law that was soon applied generally, the coat continued to be made with a sword flap. In the mid-nineteenth century the coatee came into fashion for the footman's undress indoor livery. This was cut on the same lines as a gentleman's dress coat but with a shorter, wider skirt, and it still had a sword flap. A surtout, or great coat, buttoning to the neck, was worn out of doors.

Late in the nineteenth century the earlier style of coat was often replaced by a version of a contemporary gentlemen's evening dress coat. It had ornamental brass buttons and was worn with a white tie. With this and with the coatee, trousers were worn instead of breeches. The breeches that were part of state, full dress and undress livery until the Victorian period were worn with white silk stockings, and menservants with under-developed calves were sometimes required to wear padding inside them to improve the shape of their legs. Out of doors, gaiters were worn over the stockings.

Where two or three footmen were kept, it was sometimes stipulated that they should be of a similar height: at Hatfield House, for instance, they had to be over 6ft. Small differences could be adjusted with the hat. After 1830, footmen wore the silk top hat that had replaced the cocked hat worn by people of quality in the eighteenth century, and hair powdered with violet powder was preferred to a curled and powdered wig. White gloves were worn at all times on duty, indoors and out.

Although a footman might be employed for his fine figure and obsequiously attentive manner, there was still his 'multifarious and incessant' business to be attended to. He worked hard below stairs to maintain standards above, and there he changed from his full or undress livery into a single-breasted pantry jacket, often of striped cotton twill.

On 1 January 1837 William Tayler began to keep a journal. He was a footman working in London for a widow, Mrs Prinsep, and her unmarried daughter, and he was the only manservant; she also kept a cook, lady's maid and housemaid. The first entry described a day typical in his life (the 'boys' were visitors to the house): 'I got up at half past seven, cleaned the boys' clothes and knives [and] lamps, got the parlour breakfast, lit my pantry fire, cleared breakfast and washed it away, dressed myself, went to church, came back got parlour lunch, had my own dinner, sit by the fire and red the Penny Magazine and opened the door when any visitors came. At 4 o'clock had my tea, took the lamps and candles up into the drawing room, shut the shutters, took glass, knives, plate and settera into the dining room, layed the cloth for dinner, took the dinner up at 6 o'clock, waited at dinner, brought the things down again at seven, washed them up, brought it down at half past, washed up, had my supper at nine, took down the lamps and candles at half past ten and went to bed at eleven'.

Duties varied from one household to another, depending partly on their size. When two or more footmen were kept, the head footman was on hall duty to answer the door to callers while the second

footman went out on foot or with the carriage; when there was only one footman, he went out and the butler answered the door. The first footman was usually regarded as the lady's footman; at dinner he stood behind his mistress's chair and throughout the day paid particular attention to her needs. Another footman might be assigned to nursery duties.

In country households where there was no odd man, the most junior footman sometimes brought in the coal, chopped the kindling wood and pumped and drew the water. Mrs Purefoy, living in Buckinghamshire between 1735 and 1753, wanted 'a footman to work in the garden, lay the cloth, wait at table and go to cart with Thomas when he is ordered, or do any other business hee is ordered to do, and not too large sized a man that hee may not be too great a load for an horse when he rides'. Besides seeing to the fires and lamps in the downstairs rooms, looking to the supplies of writing paper, nibs, ink and pounce and ironing the newspapers (which was one of his early morning duties), putting out chimney fires, clearing drains and unfreezing pipes, helping to stock the ice-house, clearing the snow from the pavement around a town house – a fine was exacted in the nineteenth century if this were not done by ten o'clock – and pursuing rats and other vermin were all jobs for which the footman had to be prepared.

Lamp trimming, another of the footman's morning jobs, was usually done in a room set aside for the purpose. There the lamps were kept on shelves during the daytime, partly because there was always a danger that the lamps would be upset, causing the fuel to leak, and partly because in lamps with glass founts the glass was liable to expand unevenly in the sun and crack. With lamps burning paraffin or colza oil (a vegetable oil in use before the introduction of paraffin in the 1860s), the footman was instructed to clean the fount with hot water and dry it carefully before refilling, making sure to use a funnel for this operation to avoid spillage.

Various methods were recommended for cleaning plate and cutlery. Of steel knives and forks James Williams wrote in *The Footman's Guide*, 'These essential articles of domestic use, being in daily wear, afford the means of showing off a servant's care to great advantage; for as they come under the observance of all the members of the family, their always coming to the table, clean, sharp and free from notches, must bespeak the good opinion of those whose commendation it should be his wish to obtain.' Steel knives were usually cleaned on a board covered with reversed leather; and steel forks with fine gravel, brickdust or sand mixed with hay.

Patent knife-cleaning machines were introduced in the 1870s and 1880s – Kent's rotary, for example, in 1882. Knives were inserted into holes in the outside edge of a narrow vertical drum-shaped wooden case, screwed by its cast-frame to bench or table, and a handle turned a series of brushes inside. Emery powder was poured on to the brushes through another hole in the top and, as the handle was turned, first the tips and then the whole blades were inserted to be polished. A model produced by Spong & Co. was known by the trade name the 'Servant's Friend'. Even with this machine, however, it was sometimes necessary to finish the cleaning by hand on a board because the brushes did not reach the blades close to where they joined the handles. The knife machine was usually kept in a room on its own because of the dust it created. The invention of stainless steel in the 1920s put an end in most households to the business and mess of cleaning knives.

There were various notions about the most effective and least harmful methods of cleaning silver. Mrs Beeton's instructions were to 'Wash the plate well to remove all grease, in a strong lather of common yellow soap and boiling water, and wipe it dry; then mix as much hartshorn powder as will be required, into a thick paste, with cold water or spirits of wine; smear this lightly over the plate with a piece of soft rag, and leave it for some time to dry. When perfectly dry, brush it off quite clean with a soft plate-brush, and polish the plate with a dry leather'. Hartshorn powder – harts' antlers, ground or flaked, were once the principal source of ammonia – was sometimes mixed with whiting (ground chalk) and water to make a thicker paste. Hand-rouging was done by rubbing red cream made from finely powdered rust and water on to an article until all the scratches were removed. Afterwards it was washed and dried and polished with a chamois leather. Rouging gave a rich, reddish glow to the silver, but it was hard on a footman's hands as most of the rubbing with rouge was done with the fingers.

The washing up was done in oval wooden bowls with hoops round them to hold the staves together. To keep them watertight, the bowls were left with a little water in them to prevent the wood from shrinking. Sinks and draining boards were lined with lead to reduce the chances of an accidental knock chipping or cracking china or glass. Soft soap was beaten to a lather with a whisk before being added to water softened with soda, and the glass, china and plate were generally washed with a sponge and rinsed in hot water before being dried with linen cloths known as 'pantry rubbers'. Particular care was taken in washing knives, as hot water was liable to crack ivory handles and soften the resin attaching the handles to the blades.

According to James Williams in *The Footman's Guide*, 'It is generally understood to be the peculiar duty of the men-servants to look after the cleaning and dusting of the tables, sideboard, chairs, trays, and all other articles of mahogany furniture in the parlour or drawing room.' He follows this up with a comment that must often have been made by the upper to the lower servants: 'be assured, whatever you may have heard to the contrary, that *arm-oil*, or *elbow-grease*, is the finest thing in the world for giving and preserving a fine polish'.

The furniture was generally moved into the middle of the room for polishing to avoid marking the walls, and metal mounts, locks and handles were always cleaned first. Gilded pictures and mirror frames were sometimes rubbed with garlic, onions or leeks to deter flies.

The footman was responsible for laying the dining-room table, carrying up the food, course by course, on wooden trays and placing them on trestles outside the dining-room door in a warming cupboard – the combination of the wooden tray and trestle were known as a butler's tray – waiting at table and clearing away afterwards. 'In first-rate establishments, the cloth is laid by the Footman, as are the knives, forks and glasses; but the Butler attends to the Plate, and

DINER À LA RUSSE.

sees that the several articles are rightly placed on the table' *(The Servants' Guide and Family Manual).*

For breakfast in the late Victorian period 'a fine damask table-cloth is laid over a baize or cloth cover; a plate, two small knives and two small forks are placed for each person, the serviette is folded mitre shape and stands on the plate, small glass cream-jugs and sugar basins for the use of two persons are placed the length of the table ... urn or teapot stands worked in beads or Berlin wool are bad style on a breakfast table, the stands are either of silver, electro-plate or china ...The sideboard is covered with a cloth, rows of knives, forks, and tablespoons, one or two dozen plates are placed upon it, also the cold viands, tongue, ham, game-pies, potted meat, and the like; the hot viands are placed upon a side table, such as eggs and bacon, dressed fish, kidneys, cutlets, boiled chicken, savoury omelette, roast partridges. These things are served in silver dishes with hot water, or spirit lamp, beneath.'

Plates and serving dishes were taken by the footman from the pantry to the kitchen to be warmed before serving. When serving lunch or dinner *á la russe*, the footman held the serving dish in his left hand, protected from the heat of a hot dish by a napkin, and offered it on the left side of the person seated at the table. His right hand was held behind his back. Drinks were served from the right when the glasses were filled at the table and not at the sideboard. It was usual to start with the lady of the house, if the family were eating alone, or with the guest on the right of the host.

'During dinner each person's knife, fork, plate, and spoon should be changed as soon as he has done with it', instructed Mrs Beeton, 'the vegetables and sauces belonging to the different dishes presented without remark to the guests; and the footman should tread lightly in moving around, and, if possible, should bear in mind, if there is a wit or humorist of the party, whose good things keep the table in a roar, that they are not expected to reach his ears'.

The footman was expected to remain expressionless whatever the subject or tone of the conversation, apparently uninterested in any sporting or financial tip that might reach his ears – and that he might use to his own advantage later – and unnoticing of the looks that passed between the diners. William Tayler noted with some disgust in his journal how ladies dressed to attract gentlemen and had 'Plenty of false haire and teeth and paint', of which he had a close view. He also reported some particularly ludicrous dinner-table talk: 'happening to have some cheese that had no colouring in it, one old lady ask the other what was the reason of some Cheese being white and others red? "Why, says one, "when the Cows eat a good many flowers, the Cheese is red, and when it's winter and they cannot get at flowers, the Cheese is white". I believe many other cockneys are quite as ignorant as these old ladies', he commented. He also remarked disapprovingly on a familiar class of conversation indulged in by ladies over the tea table, who complained of their servants and tradespeople and set to damage the reputation of one or other of a betrothed couple by industriously woven lies and malicious exaggeration.

Afternoon tea demanded a similar attention to detail. The footman placed a low table in front of the lady of the house before bringing in the tea-tray. The teaset was kept in the housekeeper's room, where the tea was usually made, and the footman brought the silver teapot, tea-kettle, sugar basin, milk jug and teaspoons from the pantry. Bread and butter, thinly sliced, scones and cakes were collected from the still room.

'The footman does not return to take away the tea-tray until the drawing-room bell is rung for him to do so, or until his mistress has left the drawing-room; but he enters the drawing-room for the purpose of placing a table in readiness for tea. He would not inform his mistress as to the reason of his entering the room, but would perform his duty in silence; neither would he knock at bed-room and dressing-room doors before entering the rooms; but at drawing-rooms, dining-rooms, boudoirs, and library-doors, it would not be so' *(the Servants' Practical Guide)*. It was the job of the footman to know how many were present in the drawing-room and how many teacups would be required.

The same servants' guide describes the different arrangements for afternoon 'At Homes' or large five o'clock teas served in the dining-room, and for lawn-tennis parties and garden-parties, when tea was often served in a marquee on the lawn. While the ladies drank tea, the gentlemen were served wine and fruit cups by the butler and footman.

The footman on carriage duty gave directions to the coachman and rode on the box with him. On arrival he rang or knocked to enquire whether the lady or gentleman were at home and – if they were, he let down the steps and opened the carriage door. During the visit he was entertained to beer and gossip in the servants' hall. If they were not at home, he would leave a visiting card. 'In going out with the carriage, the footman should be dressed in his best livery, his shoes and stockings being very clean, and his hat, great coat, &c. being well brushed; nothing being so disgraceful as a slovenly exterior. He should be ready at receiving directions at the carriage door, and accurate in delivering them to the coachman, and though he may indicate the importance of his family by his style of knocking at a door, he ought to have some regard to the nerves of the family and the peace of the neighbourhood. When the carriage waits at routs or public places, he should abstain from drinking with other servants, and take care to be within call when wanted. His expertness in letting down the steps and putting them up again, and his caution in shutting the door, so as not to injure any one, or the dresses of the ladies, are expected' *(The Complete Servant).*

Later in the nineteenth century the footman accompanying his master or mistress by railway reserved the seats – first class for them and second class for himself – and each time the train stopped ran forward along the platform to enquire whether his services were required. He carried wraps and footwarmers, a hamper of food and drinks and perhaps candle lamps that could be attached by prongs to the upholstered seats.

It was the footman's duty to sound the dressing bell half an hour before dinner and sound the bell again shortly before dinner was announced. In the evening he closed the shutters and brought in the candle or lamps or lit the gas. When it was time for the ladies and gentlemen to retire, in the days before gas and electric lighting, he stood at the foot of the staircase handing them lighted candles.

In the eighteenth century it was the custom to send a footman on ahead to occupy seats at the theatre before the arrival of his employers. When the gentlemen and their ladies eventually chose to make their appearance, the servant took himself upstairs to the gallery where he was allowed free or reduced-price admission to cheer and jeer with his friends. Servants eventually lost this privilege through their unruly behaviour.

His other perquisites included tips, or vails as they were commonly called in the eighteenth century, and at that time openly solicited from callers and guests. If this failed, they could resort to blackmail: callers were misinformed as to whether the master or mistress were at home, messages mislaid and guests with a reputation for meanness punished with the poorest service. In houses where there was gaming, card money, worth two or three times the cost of a pack of cards, was almost always paid to the footman who provided them.

In 1760 Jonas Hanway produced a pamphlet deploring the custom of giving vails, which he dedicated to the Duke of Newcastle.

This was well received; so much so that the young George III, with the encouragement of the Duke of Newcastle, forbade the acceptance of vails in the Royal Household. His example was soon followed despite the rebellious fury of importunate servants up and down the country – understandably, for upper servants in houses where there was much entertaining had been receiving as much as four times their wage in vails. Attached to a modest household, Tayler, who was paid £42 a year, received nonetheless £10 or £15 in vails in 1837. During the reign of Edward VII the practice of extravagant tipping – at best generous, at worst socially competitive – was briefly revived.

In settling accounts and carrying out transactions with tradespeople on his master's or mistress's behalf, a footman often earned himself a commission. There was always the possibility that he might influence his employers in moving their business elsewhere, and any trader, from the supplier of coals to the master's tailor, was prepared to come to a small financial arrangement with a gentleman's servant. Even if the master or mistress paid the bill, hoping to deprive his servant of a commission, the servant could call the next day to collect his percentage.

A footman was usually given two new suits of full dress livery and perhaps two undress suits a year. After a year they were deemed his property, to dispose of as he wished. A servant's wages included his board and lodging and, if beer, tea and sugar allowance were not provided, an extra sum was generally paid as an allowance. When the family was away, board wages were paid to cover the cost of food and other living expenses. In 1825, the Adams recommended 10s. 0d. a week for female servants and 12s. 0d. for male servants. In addition, the men were to be allowed a pot of ale each day and the women a pint, as well as table beer.

Board wages were a necessity rather than a perquisite, but many servants, by relying on the hospitality offered in the servants' halls and kitchens of other households, managed to save their weekly allowance. Some footmen spent it in taverns, copying the less gentle habits of their masters; other saved enough to set up as small traders. According to Dean Swift, a servant's money, combined with his smart manners and appearance, could buy him a commission in the Army.

'The life of a gentleman's servant is something like that of a bird shut up in a cage', wrote William Tayler in his journal. 'The bird is well housed and fed but is deprived of liberty, and liberty is the dearest and sweetest object of all Englishmen'. But in that same entry he conceded that there was money to be made in service if a person was lucky in getting a good place and began young. 'If a person wish to see life, I would advise him to be a gentlemen's servant. They will see high and low life, above stairs as well as life below. They will see and know more than any other class of people in the world'.

The Footman's Instructions and Receipts

PLATE POWDER

Whitening well purified from sand, applied wet, and rubbed till dry, is one of the cheapest and best of all plate powder. Various of these are mixed with ingredients highly injurious to the plate, rendering it brittle, and liable to break with a fall. If, however, the plate be boiled in water with a little powdered hartshorn, dried by the fire, and afterwards rubbed with dry soft rags which have been steeped in the liquor, it will restore its brightness, and its lustre may be increased by rubbing it with leather. Brass locks, and other articles may be cleaned in the same way.

The Housekeeper's Receipt Book, 1813

TO PACK GLASS OR CHINA

Procure some soft straw or hay to pack them in, and if they are to be sent a long way, and are heavy, the hay or straw should be a little damp, which will prevent them slipping about. Let the largest and heaviest things be always put undermost in the box or hamper. Let there be plenty of straw, and pack the articles tight.

Samuel and Sarah Adams, *The Complete Servant*, 1825

TO REMOVE EGG STAINS ON SILVER OR PLATE

Eggs have the peculiar property of turning silver of a black hue; this can easily be removed by rubbing the spoon or other article with a little salt between the finger and thumb.

James Williams, *The Footman's Guide*

TO CLEAN GLASS BOTTLES THAT HAVE HAD OIL IN THEM

Place ashes in each bottle, and immerse in cold water, then heat the water gradually until it boils; after boiling an hour let them remain till cold. Then wash the bottles in soapsuds, and rinse in clear water.

Things a Woman Wants to Know

CEMENT FOR CHINA, GLASS, &C.

To a quarter of an ounce of gum mastic add as much spirits of wine as will dissolve it. Soak a quarter of an ounce of isinglass in water till it is quite soft; then dissolve it in rum or brandy till of the consistence of glue. To this add one drachm of gum ammoniac, well rubbed and mixed. Put now the two mixtures together in a vessel over a gentle heat till properly united, and the cement is ready for use. It should be kept in a phial well corked, and when about to be used, to be set in boiling water to soften.

The Housekeeper, 1876

ADMIRABLE WAY OF CLEANING SILVER PLATE

Put your plate into some strong lees, made of pearl-ashes, wherein half an ounce of cream of tartar and the like quantity of alum has been dissolved; set it over the fire, let it boil five or six minutes, then take out your plate; let it dry either in the sun, or by the fire, and afterwards rub it with a soft leather, and ashes of burnt wheat straw. By this means the plate looks like new, and remains so a long time, but where time will not permit to do as above directed, you may clean with the ashes only.

The School of Arts; or, Fountain of Knowledge

PLATE-RAGS FOR DAILY USE

Boil soft rags (nothing is better for the purpose than the tops of old cotton stockings) in a mixture of new milk and hartshorn powder, in the proportion of 1 oz. of powder to a pint of milk; boil them for 5 minutes; wring them as soon as they are taken out, for a moment, in cold water, and dry them before the fire. With these rags rub the plate briskly as soon as it has been well washed and dried after daily use. A most beautiful deep polish will be produced, and the plate will require nothing more than merely to be dusted with a leather or a dry soft cloth, before it is again put on the table.

Mrs Isabella Beeton, *The Book of Household Management*, 1861

TO MAKE THE CELEBRATED FRENCH POLISH FOR FURNITURE

If the article to be polished has been previously waxed, it must be cleaned off with glass paper. To one pint of spirits of wine, add two ounces of gum shellac, and half an ounce of gum sandrach; place the whole over a gentle fire, frequently agitating it till the gums are dissolved. Then make a roller of list, put a little of the mixture upon it, and cover that with a soft linen rag, which must be slightly touched with cold-drawn linseed oil. Rub them into the wood in a circular direction, covering only a small space at a time, till the pores of the wood are filled up. After this, rub in, in the same manner, spirits of wine, with a small portion of the polish added to it, and the effect will be complete.

The Modern Family Receipt Book, 1831

TO HARDEN QUILLS

In order to harden a quill that is soft, thrust the barrel into hot ashes, stirring it till it is soft; and then taking it out, press it almost flat upon your knee with the back of a pen-knife, and afterwards reduce it to a roundness with your fingers. Another method to harden quills is by setting water and alum over the fire, and while it is boiling put in a handful of quills, the barrel only, for a minute, and then lay them by.

The School of Arts; or, Fountain of Knowledge

TO COLOUR THE BARRELS OF QUILLS

Take a pint of vinegar, and put in half an ounce of alum, powdered vermillion and brazil, of each one ounce; boil it till the liquor thickens; then strain it, and put the liquor into a narrow deep skillet; when it boils, hold the quills in the liquor till the colour has struck.

To tinge them yellow, take one pennyworth of saffron, and one ounce of turmeric in powder, boiled in vinegar as above.

The School of Arts; or, Fountain of Knowledge

TO MAKE BLACK SEALING WAX

Take bees'-wax one pound, rosin powdered one ounce, turpentine three ounces, oil of olives one ounce; mix and melt them together, to which add lamp or ivory black; and when cool, make it into what form you please.

The School of Arts; or, Fountain of Knowledge

SUBSTITUTE FOR INDIAN INK

Boil parchment slips, or cuttings of glove leather, in water till it forms a size which, when cool, becomes of the consistence of jelly; then having blackened an earthen plate, by holding it over the flame of a candle, mix up with a camel hair pencil, the fine lamp black thus obtained with some of the above size, while the plate is still warm. This black requires no grinding, and produces an ink of the very colour, which works as freely with the pencil, and is perfectly transparent, as the best Indian ink; it possesses the advantage of furnishing artists with a substitute for that article, which can be prepared in situations where it may be difficult to obtain the ink itself.

The School of Arts; or, Fountain of Knowledge

QUILLS PREPARED FOR WRITING

Quills may be hardened for use by dipping them for a minute in some boiling water in which alum has been dissolved, or by thrusting them into hot ashes till they become soft, and afterwards pressing and scraping them with the back of a knife. When they are to be clarified, the barrels are to be scraped and cut at the end, and then put into boiling water for a quarter of an hour, with a quantity of alum and salt. Afterwards they are dried in an oven, or in a pan of hot sand.

The Housekeeper's Receipt Book, 1813

TO MAKE A BEAUTIFUL BLUE WRITING INK

Take half a pint of elderberry juice into a glass vessel, put in some powdered alum, and half a quarter of a pint of vinegar and a very little urine; stir it well and try if the colour is good by dipping in a piece of white linen rag; if too pale add a little more elderberry juice, and if too dark add a little more vinegar.

The School of Arts; or, Fountain of Knowledge

LIGHTING WAX CANDLES

If you have occasion at times to light a considerable number while, perhaps, a part of the company are present, in such case previously touch the wicks with a little spirits of wine by means of a small camel-hair painting-brush, or by any other ready plan, and they will catch the flame the instant it is applied to them. If your wax candles get dirty, or appear yellow at any time, rub them with a piece of flannel dipped in spirits of wine, which will clean and restore them to their original colour.

James Williams, *The Footman's Guide*

FASTENING ON KNIFE-HANDLES

Set the handle upon end, fill the cavity with pulverised rosin, then warm the small part of the knife or fork and insert it slowly, push it down firmly, and hold it in right position until the rosin cools enough to set. As rosin is not soluble in water, hot or cold, the knives are not loosened.

The Housekeeper, 22 April 1876

TO PREPARE A FLOOR FOR A DANCE

To prepare a floor for a dance, it should be swept and scrubbed, and then, when dry, well sprinkled with powdered boracic acid, which should be rubbed in thoroughly. The children of the house may with advantage be allowed to dance on it, or to slide up and down, for nothing polishes a floor better than a few pairs of active feet.

Things a Woman Wants to Know

TO CLEAN CANDLESTICKS AND SNUFFERS

If silver or plated, care must be taken that they are not scratched in getting off the wax or grease; therefore never use a knife for that purpose, nor hold them before the fire to melt the wax or grease, as in general the hollow part of the candlesticks, towards the bottom, is filled with a composition that will melt if made too hot. Pour boiling water over them; this will take all the grease off without injury, if wiped directly with an old cloth, and save the brushes from being greased; let them in all other respects be cleaned like the rest of the plate.

Be very particular in cleaning the patent snuffers, as they go with a spring, and are easily broken. The part which shuts up the snuffings has in general a small hole in it, where a pin can be put in to keep it open while cleaning it; be sure to have them well cleaned, that the snuff may not drop about when using them. The extinguishers likewise must be cleaned in the inside, and put ready with the snuffers, that the candlesticks may not be taken up without them.

Samuel and Sarah Adams, *The Complete Servant*, 1825

TO PREVENT THE SMOKING
OF A LAMP

Soak the wick in strong vinegar, and dry it well before you use it; it will then burn both sweet and pleasant, and give much satisfaction for the trifling trouble in preparing it.

If for want of the above mentioned preparation any should escape, a wet sponge suspended by a string or wire over the flame of a lamp, at a few inches distance, will absorb all the smoke and disagreeable effluvia. Rince it in warm water when wanted the next day.

Samuel and Sarah Adams, *The Complete Servant*, 1825

CRUST PREVENTED IN TEA KETTLES

Hard water used for tea is apt to form an offensive crust with-inside the tea-ket-tle, which might be prevented by fre-quent cleaning, or putting a flat oyster shell at the bottom; this will attract the stony particles that are in the water, and the concretion will be formed upon it.

The Housekeeper's Receipt Book, 1813

TO DESTROY RATS

A number of corks must be cut down as thin as sixpences, and stewed in grease, and then placed in the way of the rats. They will greedily devour this special recipe, and will die of indigestion.

The Housewife's Receipt-Book, 1837

TO MANAGE WATER-PIPES IN WINTER

When the frost begins to set in, cover the water-pipes with hay or straw bands, twisted tight round them. Let the cisterns and water butts be washed out occasionally; this will keep the water pure and fresh.

In pumping up water into the cistern for the water closet, be very particular, in win-ter-time, as in general the pipes go up the outside of the house. Let all the water be let out of the pipe when you have done pump-ing; but if this be forgotten, and it should get frozen, take a small gimblet and saw a *hole* in the pipe, a little distance from the place where it is let off, which will prevent its bursting. Put a peg in to the hole, when the water is let off. Pump the water up into the cistern, for the closet every morning, and once a week take a pail of water, and cast it into the basin, having first opened the trap at the bottom; this will clear the soil out of the pipe.

Samuel and Sarah Adams, *The Complete Servant*, 1825

The Valet

Loyalty, courtesy and discretion were the qualities required of a good valet. Of the last quality *The Complete Servant* had this to say: 'As the valet is much about his master's person, and has the opportunity of hearing his off-at-hand opinions on many subjects, he should endeavour to have as short a memory as possible, and above all keep his master's council; and he should be very cautious of mischief-making or tale-bearing to the prejudice of other persons, as calculated to involve his master in disputes, and ruin himself if by chance he is incorrect'.

In the opinion of Mrs Beeton, the valet was in no position to pass judgment on his master's behaviour, due to his imperfect education, but, as his master's confidant, his advice might often be sought on amorous as well as sartorial matters. 'The valet and waiting-maid are placed near the persons of the master and mistress, receiving orders only from them, accompanying them in all their journeys; the confidants and agents of their most unguarded moments; of their most secret habits, and of course subject to their commands – even to their caprices'. In the service of those who are 'from sheer wealth, station and education, more polished and consequently more susceptible of annoyance', patience, a modest demeanour and a respectful reserve were essential.

The valet was not found in every household. In those of gentlemen who seldom left the country his duties would often be performed by the butler or a footman. For the socially inclined bachelor, however, who travelled and paid country-house visits, a valet was indispensable; he was also often found in the households of elderly gentlemen and in those where sixteen or more indoor servants were kept.

Despite the close relationship between master and valet, the personal servant's status in the household gradually declined as time went by. In the Middle Ages he would have been the son of a knight or a nobleman, employed as much for his own education as to serve his master, and even in the early nineteenth century he still ranked above the butler. He became known as the 'gentleman's gentleman' and his master's cast-off clothes contributed to his gentlemanly, if often rather old-fashioned, appearance.

It was not only his clothes, however, that set him apart from the rest of the servants. The nature of his position would take him abroad, to London and to the houses of his master's friends. He thus acquired a familiarity with Society and the wider world; moreover, he alone had access to the master at all times, and as a result the other servants tended to regard him with respect and even wariness. In *The Servant's Guide and Family Manual* the duties of the valet are described as follows: 'His especial business is to attend to the personal accommodation of his master; to take care of his entire wardrobe; and to attend to the general business of the dressing-room'. Before the master rose in the morning his boots and shoes would be cleaned – perhaps with a blacking of the valet's own concoction – and his clothes brushed. Meanwhile, the housemaid would have cleaned and dusted the dressing-room and lit the fire. The valet would then prepare the washing-stand; brushes – hair, nail and tooth – had to be in their proper places, and hot water in the ewer. Dressing-gown and slippers would be laid to warm in front of the fire.

Before about 1820 clothes were kept in presses laid flat. Hence, the detailed instructions given in *The Complete Servant*: 'The coat, trowsers, &c. intended to be worn must be taken out and placed at length across the backs of chairs, the sleeves and outsides turned inward, with a clean linen or brown Holland wrapper thrown over them, to save them from dust… The best way to hang up a coat is, to fold it once at full length, with the inside outward, the sleeves put straight, and the two fronts together, and then hang it on a cloak pin by the inside of the shoulder.'

Although most gentlemen shaved themselves, the valet might be required to do so, particularly if his master were old or infirm. Hair and beard would also have to be trimmed, or, sometimes, encouraged by the application of the patent potions such as were advertised frequently on the front pages of *The Times* in the nineteenth century. A sharp razor was essential and stropping it was a matter of skill: the blade was first washed and dried and then drawn diagonally, from the heel to the point, down the length of the strop, the elbow being moved in and out each time the blade was reversed.

In the late morning and before dinner, the valet might be expected to carry out various secretarial duties. He kept account of visitors and tried to make sure that their calls were returned by his master. He was responsible for all travelling arrangements, and for this purpose a smattering of French and other foreign languages – convincing to his master if no-one else – was regarded as useful. In the nineteenth century, as the railway extended throughout the length and breadth of Britain, he learnt to consult his *Bradshaw*.

'In this wandering age, when ladies explore pyramids, and gentlemen propose to visit the North Pole upon dandy accelerators, it may not be uninteresting to know how six months' provisions can be packed up in a reticle, or a cream-pot replenished in Spitzbergen', wrote the author of *A New System of Practical Domestic Economy*, published in 1824. There follows a recipe for a vegetable compound 'by which persons engaged in exploring hot and desart regions, may be saved from perishing by hunger and thirst'. The ingredients were jelly made from starch with boiling water, gum arabic, catechu (obtained from certain trees and shrubs in the East) and citric acid — one wonders if it were ever put to the test.

The servant accompanying an English gentleman on the Continent would not expect to encounter the same difficulties as a traveller to the North Pole or the desert, but he did have to deal with Customs authorities, bargain for the best accommodation and food, and procure the best horses or a corner seat in a railway carriage. He had to be able to detect contaminated water and get rid of bed bugs. Some knowledge of medicine was also important as foreign doctors were suspected to be even less trustworthy than their English counterparts.

For many Victorian gentlemen, the winter months were punctuated by frequent visits to friends and relations to shoot game. From being an informal affair with two dogs and a fowling-piece, shooting became an important part of the social life of the upper classes, and in this the valet had his part to play. Clad in tweeds and a bowler hat, he would stand behind his master in the field, armed with the second gun, loaded and ready to be passed deftly when the first had been discharged. It was a task that required quite as much skill as wielding a razor, and was just as likely to earn abuse if it were inefficiently done.

Luncheon would be brought out and eaten at trestle tables set up in a barn or cottage, and the valet would assist the footman in serving it, paying particular attention to the needs of his master. In his room at the end of the day the valet might prepare a mustard bath for his master's feet or rub him down with *eau de Cologne* to prevent his taking a chill.

A day's hunting meant a day at home, for horses were not the valet's affair. But the master's return brought a long evening's work: boots caked with mud had to be dried and cleaned, ready for boning and polishing the following day. Hunting coats had to be sponged down, silk hats brushed and ironed and breeches dried and cleaned and the chamois leather seat and inside legs carefully coated with a yellow paste known as 'breeches' ball'.

At dinner the valet would be required to act as an extra footman, serving his master and standing behind his chair. Like all servants whose duties included waiting at table, he would be expected to maintain an impassive expression and to have 'no ears'.

In the servants' hierarchy the valet was numbered among the 'Upper Ten'. Just as in his master's house he would take the latter part of all his meals in the housekeeper's room (or, in particularly grand houses, in the steward's room), so when visiting as his master's servant, the same privilege would be extended to him. The rules of precedence were applied among the upper servants just as strictly as they were in the dining-room above.

Thus, the valet of a visiting duke would be seated in a place which reflected the superiority of his master's rank. This was likely to be on the housekeeper's right, unless of course, there were a royal servant present, or in the days of sporting clergymen, the servant of an archbishop. Formality below stairs was such that in some houses visiting personal servants were required to wear evening dress, and if they were unable to do so, were relegated to the company of the lower servants in the servants' hall. On visits such as this the loyalty and discretion of the valet were put to their severest test as he gossiped with his equals over the butler's port.

But devotion takes many forms. Lady Violet Greville, in the *National Review* of February 1892, remarked on a particular paradox she had noted amongst the best kind of valet: 'If he smokes your cigars, your loose cash may lie about freely; he will not touch it. You who are so careless with your studs and sleeve-links possess an attendant who counts and looks after them. If he occasionally helps himself to a glass or two of wine, he pays your bills punctually, and in order'.

The Valet's Instructions and Receipts

EAU DE COLOGNE

Into 2 quarts spirits of wine at 36, put 2 drachms essence of bergamot, the same of essence of cedrat (a superior kind of bergamot), 2 drachms essence of citron, 1 oz. essence of rosemary, and a 1/4 drachm of the essence of neroly (an oil produced from the flowers of the Seville orange tree): let it stand twenty-four hours, then strain through brown paper, and bottle it.

Anne Cobbett, *The English Housekeeper*, 1842

NOTIONS FOR TRAVELLERS

Never use leather straps to trunks which have to go through the Custom House, but instead cord the boxes with the thickest and strongest rope that can be obtained, and knot them with inextricable knots, and give a dab of tar or oil on the knots. The officials have a great hatred of them, and out of pity for their own fingers let these trunks alone, and pass on to those fastened with straps.

Mrs de Salis, *Wrinkles and Notions for Every Household*, 1890

TO TAKE OUT GREASE FROM CLOTHES

Have a hot iron with some thick brown paper; lay the paper on the part where the grease is, then put the iron upon the spot; if the grease comes through the paper, put another piece, till it does not soil the paper. If not all out, wrap a little bit of cloth or flannel round the finger, dip it into spirit of wine, and rub the grease spot; this will take it entirely out. Be careful not to have the iron too hot; but try it on a piece of white paper, and if it turn the paper brown, or scorch it in the least, it is too hot. If paint should get on the coats, always have spirit of wine or turpentine ready, which, with a piece of flannel or cloth, will easily take it off, if not left to get quite dry.

Samuel and Sarah Adams, *The Complete Servant*, 1825

TO MAKE BLACKING

Take of ivory black and treacle, each 12 oz., spermaceti oil, 4 oz., white wine vinegar, 4 pints.
Mix. This blacking, (recommended by Mr. Gray, lecturer on the materia medica,) is superior in giving leather a finer polish than any of those that are advertised, as they all contain sulphuric acid, (oil of vitriol,) which is necessary, to give it the polishing quality, but it renders leather rotten and very liable to crack.

Samuel and Sarah Adams, *The Complete Servant*, 1825

TO TAKE GREASE OUT OF LEATHER BREECHES

The white of an egg applied to the injured part, and dried in the sun, will effectually answer this purpose.

Another Method

To two table spoonsful of spirit of turpentine, put half one ounce of mealy potatoes, add some of the best Durham mustard, with a little vinegar; let them dry, and when well rubbed, the spots will be entirely removed.

Samuel and Sarah Adams, *The Complete Servant*, 1825

A BLACK VARNISH FOR GENTLEMEN'S OLD STRAW OR CHIP HATS

Take best black sealing wax, half an ounce; rectified spirit of wine, two ounces; powder the sealing wax, and put it in with the spirit of wine, into a four ounce phial; digest them in a sand heat, or near a fire, till the wax is dissolved; lay it on warm with a fine soft hair brush, before a fire, or in the sun. It gives a good stiffness to old straw hats, and a beautiful gloss equal to new, and resists wet. If the hats are very brown, they may be brushed over with writing ink, and dried before the varnish is applied. Spirit of turpentine may probably be used in the place of the spirit of wine.

The School of Arts; or, Fountain of Knowledge

TO RENDER BOOTS, SHOES, AND OTHER LEATHER ARTICLES, WATERPROOF

Linseed oil, a quarter of a pint; mutton (kidney) suet, two ounces; rosin, one ounce; – Boil the oil in a glazed pipkin, over a slow fire; pound the rosin, and add it to the oil; and cut the suet into small pieces, and add it to the rest. When well mixed, it is ready for use. Be careful not to let this boil over, which it is very likely to do, or it will set the chimney ablaze in a moment. Lay the mixture over the boot or shoe, with a sponge or soft brush, while yet warm.

...The next morning, the boot or shoe may be blacked for wearing, if the mixture remains on the surface of the leather, it may scraped off, previous to cleaning.

James Williams, *The Footman's Guide*

SQUEAKING BOOTS

The remedy for these is to boil linseed oil. Pour into a deep dish and place the boots in it, so as to allow the oil to saturate the soles thoroughly for a few days. If this does not remove the annoyance, repeat the process.

Things a Woman Wants to Know

TO CLEAN BUTTONS

Buttons are cleaned by putting them in a board made on purpose, with a slit in it, to prevent the coat being dirtied, and rubbing them with a sponge dipped in moistened whitening if white ones, or in rottenstone or plate-powder for brass or yellow ones, and polishing them with a soft brush.

Duties of the Butler, 1858

TOOTH POWDER

3 oz. camphor, 1 oz. powdered cinchona bark, 1 oz. prepared charcoal, and sufficient sprits of wine to dissolve the camphor. Mix thoroughly, and pass through a fine sieve. – The mixture of chalk and camphor is very good for preserving as well as cleansing teeth.

Anne Cobbett, *The English Housekeeper*, 1842

HATS

Gentlemen's hats are often damaged by a shower of rain, which takes off the gloss and leaves them spotted. To prevent this, shake out the wet as much as possible, wipe the hat carefully with a clean handkerchief, observing to lay the beaver smooth; then fix the hat in its original shape, and hang it at a distance from the fire to dry. Next morning, brush it several times with a soft brush in the proper direction, and the hat will have sustained but little injury. A flat iron moderately heated, and passed two or three times gently over the hat, will raise the gloss, and give the hat its former good appearance.

The Housekeeper's Receipt Book, 1813

TO PRESERVE HATS

Hats require great care, or they will soon look shabby. Brush them with a soft camel-hair brush, which will keep the fur smooth. Have a stick for each hat, to keep it in its proper shape, especially if the hat be wet: put the stick in as soon as the hat is taken off, and when dry put it into a hat-box, particularly if not in constant use, as the air and dust soon turn hats brown. If the hat is very wet, handle it as lightly as possible; wipe it dry with a cloth or silk handkerchief; then brush it with the soft brush.

Samuel and Sarah Adams, *The Complete Servant*, 1825

TO BRUSH CLOTHES

Have a wooden horse to put the clothes on, and a small cane or small hand-whip to beat the dust out of them, also a board or table long enough for them to be put their whole length when brushing them. Have two brushes, one hard and the other soft: use the hardest for the great coats, and the others when spotted with dirt. Fine cloth coats should never be brushed with too hard a brush, as this will take off the nap, and make them look bare in a little time. Be careful in the choice of your cane; do not have it too large, and be particular not to hit too hard; be careful also not to hit the buttons, for it will scratch, if not break them.

If a coat be wet, and spotted with dirt, let it be quite dry before you brush it; then rub out the spots with the hands, taking care not to rumple it. If it want beating, do it as before directed; then lay the coat at its full length on a board; let the collar be towards the left hand, and the brush in the right; brush the back of the collar first, between the two shoulders next, and then the sleeves, &c. observing to brush the cloth the same way that the nap goes, which is towards the bottom of the coat. When both sides are properly done, fold them together; then brush the inside, and last of all the collar.

Samuel and Sarah Adams, *The Complete Servant*, 1825

AN EXCELLENT WATER TO PREVENT HAIR FROM FALLING OFF AND TO THICKEN IT

Put four pounds of unadulterated honey into a still with twelve handfuls of the tendrils of vines, and the same quantity of rosemary-tops. Distil as cool and as slowly as possible. The liquor may be allowed to drop till it begins to taste sour.

A New System of Domestic Cookery, 1860

TO MANAGE RAZOR STROPS

Keep them moderately moist with a drop or two of sweet oil; a little crocus martis and a few drops of sweet oil, rubbed well in with a glass bottle, will give the razor a fine edge; pass it afterwards on the inside of your hand when warm, and dip it in hot water just before using.

Samuel and Sarah Adams, *The Complete Servant*, 1825

SHAVING SOAP

Cut half a pound of fine white soap in thin slices, and half an ounce of salt of tartar, and mix them with full half a pint of spirits of wine. Put the ingredients into a quart bottle, tie it down with a bladder, digest it in a gentle heat till the soap is dissolved, and let the air escape through a pin hole in the bladder. Filter the mixture through paper, and scent it with a little bergamot or essence of lemon. It will have the appearance of fine oil; a small quantity mixed with water will produce an excellent lather, and is much superior to any other composition in washing or shaving.

The Housekeeper's Receipt Book, 1813

TO THICKEN A MOUSTACHE

Take 1 oz. of tincture of cantharides, the same of tincture of capsicum, and 1 oz. of rosewater to make a lotion, which rub into the moustache morning and night.

Mrs de Salis, *Wrinkles and Notions for Every Household*, 1890

CURLING FLUID

Melt a bit of bees' wax about the size of a filbert kernel, slowly in 1 oz. of oil of almonds, and then add a drop or two of ottar of rose.

Anne Cobbett, *The English Housekeeper*, 1842

The Housekeeper

The housekeeper's symbol of office was the chatelaine that hung from her waist, to which were attached the keys to the still room and the linen and store cupboards. Hidden beneath her apron, traditionally worn in the nineteenth century over a high-necked dress with a brooch, and with a shawl, the keys could be heard jangling together as she went about her business, warning of her approach.

As head of the female servants, ranking beneath the house steward or on a level with the butler, she was constantly on the watch for slovenly or careless work, untidiness in the servants' appearance, undisciplined behaviour and unpunctuality. 'If the under servants could be depended on for doing all their business according to the *instructions that could be given them*', wrote Susanna Whatman in 1776, 'the eye of a Housekeeper would not be necessary to keep everything going on in its proper way. But this is never to be expected, and as the mistress of a large family can neither afford the time, nor even have it in her power, to see what her servants are about, she must depend upon the Housekeeper to see all her orders enforced and every rule kept up'. In the characteristically brisk words of Mrs Beeton, 'the housekeeper must consider herself as the immediate representative of her mistress, and bring, to the management of the household, all those qualities of honesty, industry, and vigilance, in the same degree as if she were at the head of *her own* family. Constantly on the watch to detect any wrong-doing on the part of any of the domestics, she will overlook all that goes on in the house, and will see that every department is thoroughly attended to, and that the servants are comfortable, at the same time that their various duties are properly performed'.

In the Victorian period a housekeeper was employed in the houses of the great, where there was a large female staff to supervise in the absence of a house steward, and in the town houses of the middle classes, where the mistress was inexperienced in, and scorned, domestic matters. In either case she engaged and dismissed the female staff – with the exception of the lady's maid and children's nurse, and sometimes the cook; she was accorded the courtesy title of 'Mrs', whether or not she were married; and she was addressed as 'Madam' by the lower servants as a mark of respect.

H. G. Wells in *Tono-Bungay* described the housekeeper's room as a 'much-cupboarded, white-painted, chintz-brightened' room, where the upper servants assembled. Recollecting his mother's room at Uppark, in Sussex, where he spent a part of his childhood, he listed among its contents 'an old peerage and a Crockford together with the books of recipes, the Whitaker's Almanack, the Old Moore's Almanack, and the eighteenth century dictionary, on the little dresser that broke the cupboards on one side'.

The housekeeper generally entertained the upper servants in her room, known irreverently by the lower servants as the 'Pugs' Parlour', to breakfast, tea and supper, and after the meat course at servants' hall dinner they retired there, sometimes bearing away the remnants of the joint with them. 'The general rule is for the upper and under servants to sit down to table together in the servants' hall, the upper servants being the first to enter, and for the upper servants to have the sweets and bread and cheese in the housekeeper's room.... The hot meat and vegetables are placed upon the table; and, where there are two joints provided, they are carved by the butler and housekeeper. The bread and jugs of beer are not placed on the table, but are helped by the footman as required'.

'The still-room maid lays the table in the housekeeper's room, where the upper servants adjourn to finish their dinner. The table is covered with a white table cloth; a knife and fork, dessert-spoon, and tumbler are placed for each person. The pudding or tart, or both, are brought into the housekeeper's room by the still-room maid when the servants are seated at table, and then returns to finish her own dinner: the bell is rung for her to bring in the cheese as soon as the sweet has been eaten' *(The Servants' Practical Guide)*. In households where there was a house steward a similar ritual was enacted in the steward's room, but even so, tea for the upper servants was always in the housekeeper's room.

A strict order of precedence was applied to seating arrangements in most servants' halls. The steward or butler sat at one end of the table and the housekeeper at the other. Grace was said by the most senior or the longest-serving member of the household. In the nineteenth century, the upper servants in a large establishment disdained conversing with the lower ranks even at table; their day for a napkin ring, marked with their initials, wine instead of beer and other such privileges might come, but in the meantime they should 'know their place'.

In some houses, especially in towns, the servants were required to attend church on Sunday evenings, a cold dinner having been ordered for the dining-room to enable all but a few to leave the house for an hour or so. If there were a church parade for morning

service, protocol was again observed in the order in which they entered the church, and in the country the order of precedence included the outdoor servants and villagers: 'The doctor in Bladesover ranked below the vicar but above the "vet", artists and summer visitors squeezed in above or below this point according to their appearance and expenditure, and then in a carefully arranged scale came the tenantry, the butler and housekeeper, the village shopkeeper, the head keeper, the cook, the publican, the second keeper, the blacksmith (whose status was complicated by his daughter keeping the post-office – and a fine hash she used to make of telegrams, too!), the village shopkeeper's eldest son, the first footman, younger sons of the village shopkeeper, his first assistant, and so forth' (H. G. Wells, *Tono-Bungay*).

The housekeeper generally belonged to one house, staying there while most of the other servants moved with the family when they went to another house. In their absence, she and the housemaids who were left behind occupied themselves with making and checking inventories of the household linen, furniture and china, washing and remaking the bedding, taking up the carpets and rugs and cleaning the wallpaper with breadcrumbs. Once or twice a year the house was cleaned from top to bottom under her supervision. In the spring, the accumulated dirt from the winter's fires, and from the candles and oil or gas lamps, was removed by scrubbing and polishing and the winter curtains taken down, washed and put away, to be replaced by lighter summer ones; in the autumn they were put up again. In the summer and autumn there were fruit and herbs to be picked on dry days in the country, and preserves and pickles to be made. In October and November preparations began for the cold weather and Christmas.

In some houses the linen and stores were kept in cupboards in the housekeeper's room. In larger establishments there were separate closets for the linen and stores, and a still room where medicines, toilet waters and cordials were distilled. The store cupboard, or room, was the battlefield of mice, rats and insects, with damp as the lesser ememy. Flour and grain were kept in containers on hanging shelves, and loaf sugar was tied up in paper and hung up; tea was best kept in a chest lined with lead, and coffee, once it was ground, in canisters and as far as possible from the tea to avoid tainting it.

'Soap will be the better for keeping – indeed, it should not be used when newly made. The cakes should be cut with a wire or string, into oblong squares, and laid up, on a dry shelf, a little distance apart, and across each other, so as to admit the air betwixt them, to harden it. This method will save one third' *(The Complete Servant)*. If dried quickly, soap was liable to crack and break when it was wetted. Both soap and candles were best when they were made in cold weather.

Wax candles were expensive and were therefore given out sparingly from the store cupboard. The following advice on economy was offered in *The Servants' Guide*: 'Wax candles, four in the pound, will last about eleven hours, and should be used only when the evening is expected to be five hours, as, in that case, each candle will serve for two nights. Shorter candles, of six to the pound, are preferable when required to burn six or seven hours'. Cheaper tallow candles were used in many households when there were no visitors, and they were provided for the servants. A servant found by the housekeeper with a candle alight when he or she had fallen asleep was reprehended as much for extravagance as for permitting the possibility of a fire.

Making distilled waters was one of the housekeeper's most difficult tasks. For rose water, freshly gathered petals were steeped in salt for twenty-four hours. The Adams gave instructions for making a paste for preserving the petals so that they could be used whenever they were wanted. 'Rub three pounds of rose-leaves for three minutes with a pound of common salt. The flowers being bruised by the friction of the grains of salt, form a paste, which is to be put into an earthen jar, or into a water-tight barrel. The same process is to be repeated until the vessel is filled, so that all the roses may be equally salted. The vessel is then to be shut up and kept in a cool place until wanted'. When this aromatic paste was required, it was put into a vessel with twice its weight of water.

Orange, wormwood, lavender, cinnamon, pennyroyal, mint and strawberry waters were made by bruising the flower or leaf before adding the water; 'spirituous waters' – Hungary water, Maraschino and the liqueurs used in the making of cakes, ices and conserves – were made by steeping the ingredients in spirit and adding only as much water as would prevent a burnt flavour. 'Every liqueur made by infusions, is called *ratafia*; that is, when the spirit is made to imbibe thoroughly the aromatic flavour and colour of the fruit steeped in it: when this has taken place, the liqueur is drawn off, and sugar added to it; it is then filtered and bottled' *(The Italian Confectioner)*.

Vinegar was commonly made by mixing 1 lb of honey with 1 gallon of cider and allowing it to stand for several months. It could also be made from wine, gooseberries and currants, and the Adams gave a recipe for 'Vinegar from the refuse of Bee-hives'. Its principal use was as a preservative, but the Adams recommended its use 'when an overdose of strong wine, spirit, opium or other narcotic poison has been taken. The housekeeper preserved vegetables in brine or vinegar, or made from them savoury relishes – piccalilli, chutney and ketchup – and she assisted the cook in pickling fish and meat.

Soap, cosmetics and medicines were also made by the housekeeper, often helped by the still-room maid, and in some households she made tallow and wax candles. Currants, berries and hips, plums, peaches and other soft fruits, she dried, conserved in syrup or brandy, crystallized or made into jams, jellies or cordials.

The housekeeper gathered flowers and herbs for drying, pounding the ones to be used in cooking with a pestle and mortar and putting them away in pots and bottles in her store cupboard. With the lady's maid she made fragrant essences for the lady's and gentlemen's toilet and *pot pourri*, she embroidered and filled muslin lavender bags for the linen cupboard and made herbal drinks and pomades.

Depending on the size of the household and the experience and skills of the cook, the housekeeper might take responsibility for preparing the pudding and dessert for dinner. Pastries, fruit creams, soufflés and sweet omelettes, *compôtes*, water ices and ice creams were her culinary specialities. Ice creams were made either by swirling a container in a tub of ice and salt until its contents froze to

THE SERVANTS' BALL.

the inside, or with a patent freezing machine such as was recommended in the later editions of *The Book of Household Management*. It was the housekeeper who made the muffins and scones, cakes and biscuits for afternoon tea, and who blended and made the tea. The teaset was kept in a cupboard in the housekeeper's room while the spoons and other silver articles were brought up from the pantry.

The house steward saw to the marketing, and he also collected, examined and discharged the tradesmen's bills. In the absence of a house steward, these duties devolved on the housekeeper. Meat, fish and groceries, and vegetables and fresh fruit if they were not grown on the place or sent up to town in hampers, were ordered after consultation with the cook. Each article was weighed or measured to make sure that the ticket sent with it was correct. At a desk in her room the housekeeper prepared the household accounts, which were submitted to the mistress of the house for weekly or monthly inspection.

'By giving, in the course of the year, one or two large orders to any respectable shop, and always to the same one, you may pretty well depend upon being supplied with good articles', wrote Anne Cobbett in *The English Housekeeper*; 'but not so, if you send here and there, and for small quantities at a time; besides the great inconvenience of finding yourself now and then, without the very thing which you want, and the trouble of sending every Saturday by the carrier perhaps; to say nothing of having to open the different parcels and put away their contents on a Saturday night or Sunday morning, or leave them, for a day, to the mercy of the rats and mice'. A large grocery order was valuable custom and deserved the attention of the shop's manager.

Most housekeeping manuals offered advice on testing for adulteration in foods, especially flour, on testing for freshness in fish and eggs and on the buying of fruit, vegetables and fish. Fresh fish was a luxury to all but those living near the coast until the railways brought it inland; hence the number of recipes for freshwater fish such as chub, dace and roach.

An illustration to the 1888 edition of Mrs Beeton shows some of the brands of tinned provisions and household requisites that were available at that date. Shoe blacking and Brunswick black, plate powder, furniture cream and French polish as well as cocoa, golden syrup, potted shrimps and corned beef were among the commercially prepared products with which the housekeeper could stock her store cupboard. In 1847 a meat canning factory was started in Australia, and Australian tinned meat was shown at the 1851 Great Exhibition in London. In that year a large batch of British tinned meat supplied to the Admiralty was found to be unfit for human consumption, which was a setback for the industry; however, the prejudice against tinned meat faded away when, in 1863, an epidemic of cattle disease in England raised the price of fresh meat.

As well as the keys to the store room and still room, the housekeeper kept the key to the linen cupboard. In town houses, where there was no room for a laundry or for drying and airing the linen, the washing was generally given out; in the country, in a large establishment, the laundry maids washed all the household linen and their employers' personal linen, the lady's maid, valet and nursery maid taking care of the finer garments.

The ideal laundry, according to Mrs Beeton, consisted of a washing-house and a separate room for drying and mangling, with an adjoining hot-air closet. On Monday morning the washing was sorted, examined and treated for stains and entered in a book. It was then left to soak overnight in water and soda or water and unslaked lime. The next morning the fires were lit underneath the coppers and boilers and each article removed separately from the lye in which it had been soaking, rinsed, rubbed and wrung. The vessels were then emptied and refilled with water and the articles washed with soap, this being repeated for a second wash. The linen was rinsed by boiling it with soda for an hour and a half in the copper, careful laundresses putting it in a canvas bag to protect it from the scum and the sides of the

copper; it was rinsed in hot water and again in cold water before it was wrung out. The linen was then hung up on a line or draped over sweet-smelling shrubs to dry and bleach in the sun. 'When linen is soiled and discoloured by town washing, or by age, or lying-by out of use, the best bleaching materials', according to *A New System of Practical Domestic Economy*, 'are the natural verdure of the ground, with the dews and winds of Heaven'. Thursday and Friday were the days for mangling, starching and ironing. 'The mangling process which is simply passing them between rollers subjected to a very considerable pressure, produced by weight, is confined to sheets, towels, table-linen, and similar articles, which are without folds or plaits'.

The irons described by Mrs Beeton were the common triangular and oval flat irons, heated on the stove; the box-iron, 'which is hollow, and heated by a red-hot iron inserted into the box'; and the Italian iron, 'a hollow tube, smooth on the outside, and raised on a slender pedestal with a footstalk'. This was heated with a red-hot iron inserted in the tube, and articles were drawn over the smooth outside. Crimping and gauffering machines might also be needed for collars and cuffs.

The newly washed laundry was brought to the housekeeper, who checked it and arranged it in order in the linen cupboard between bags of dried herbs and flowers. All the household linen was numbered so that each article received equal wear, dated and marked, usually in red cotton or silk, with the name or initials of the house. The housekeeper ordered the material for replacements and gave out sheets and pillowcases to the housemaids to make up the beds and to mend of an afternoon.

As the '*locum tenens*, the *Lady Bountiful*, and the active representative of the mistress of the family', the housekeeper was expected 'to do, or to see done, everything that appertains to the good and orderly management of the household' *(The Complete Servant)*. She allocated rooms to guests and the servants they brought with them and dispensed charity among the neighbouring poor on her mistress's behalf. She was also the resident adviser on medical matters; her skills were disturbingly catholic, and ranged from applying leeches (with or without the recommendation of a doctor) to remedies of her own invention for preventing hysterics.

The free time accorded to each female servant was defined at the time of her employment, but it was within the power of the house-keeper to reduce it as a punishment. In some households the visits of male acquaintances, or 'followers', was strictly forbidden. In 1880, 'The general rule is, that servants should have the opportunity of attending church once every Sunday, and twice every other Sunday, either morning, afternoon, or evening, according as the work of the house is arranged between themselves and their fellow-servants, during their temporary absence. They are also allowed one afternoon a week for going out and a whole day or half a day once a month' *(The Servants' Practical Guide)*.

The housekeeper set the tone of the household. A rigid, sarcastic spinster would more often than not bring about bad feeling below stairs; a good-natured, motherly figure – who could nonetheless impose strict discipline on the lower female servants – might create a happy atmosphere. Comfortably surrounded by mementoes of her happy life with the family and years of devotion to a house, and with a ready supply of gossip and chocolates, she could make of the housekeeper's room a cheerful meeting place for the upper servants and a refuge for members of the family from the formality of the drawing-room and the strictness of the nursery.

The Housekeeper's and Laundry Maid's Instructions and Receipts

POMADE DIVINE

Put a pound and a half of clear beef marrow into an earthenware pan of fresh water, and change the same for ten days, then steep it in rose water for 24 hours, and drain it in a cloth till dry. Take an ounce of storax, gum benjamin, odoriferous Cypress powder, or of Florence, half an ounce of cinnamon, two drachms of cloves, and two drachms of nutmeg, all finely powdered; mix them with the marrow, then put the ingredients into a three-pint pewter pot, make a paste of the white of egg and flour, and lay it upon a piece of rag, over that, put another piece of linen to cover the top close. Put the pot into a large copper pot with water, and keep it steady that it may not reach to the covering of the pot that holds the marrow. As the water shrinks, add more, for it must boil four hours without ceasing; strain the ointment through a linen cloth into small pots, and when cold cover them up close with bladder and paper. Don't touch it with anything but silver.

Samuel and Sarah Adams, *The Complete Servant*, 1825

SALINE WASH FOR HEADACHES

Take of fine salt 1/2 oz., vinegar, soft water, each 4 fluid oz., whisky or brandy, 2 fluid oz.; mix together and dissolve the salt. This is a good cooling wash in headache and inflammation of the brain. It is sometimes used tepid.

Mrs de Salis, *Wrinkles and Notions for Every Household*, 1890

SOAP

Both animal and vegetable oils are used in the manufacture of soap. The chief animal fats used are tallow, whale, and seal oils; and the chief vegetable oils are palm, linseed, and cocoa-nut oils. The alkalies employed are soda or potash. The last-named is much stronger, and when added to coarser fats, a soft, jelly-like substance is produced, which is known as *soft-soap*. This is celebrated for its sharply penetrating qualities, and hence is employed for cleansing very dirty floors or wood-work, but it seldom appears in the laundry. *Hard and compact soaps* like the common yellow, mottled and curd soaps, are made of soda, mixed with more refined fat. The curious streaks, which have given the name to the mottled variety, are caused by stirring in certain mineral matters during the cooling process. It is worth your while to remember that *soap should be purchased some time before you want to use it.* The best plan is to buy at least a bar, or about 3 lb., at a time, and cut it into squares with string, and stack the pieces so that the air can circulate round them and so dry them. A more shiftless and uneconomical practice cannot be conceived, than that of purchasing soap from the grocer as it is required, for then it is moist, and "lathers away" very quickly.

Rev. J. P. Faunthorpe (ed.), *Household Science; Reading in Necessary Knowledge for Girls and Young Women*, 1881

CAMOMILE TEA

Two dozen flowers infused in a pint of boiling water for half an hour; decant sweeten with honey, and drink half a gill – fasting.

Camomile tea, when not taken in too strong doses, from its tonic and antispasmodic qualities, strengthens the digestive organs, and tends actively to dispel dyspepsia.

C. E. Francatelli, *The Cook's Guide and Housekeeper's and Butler's Assistant*, 1877

LAVENDER WATER

Put a pound of lavender blossoms into a quart of water, and set them in a still over a slow fire; distil it off very gently till the water is all exhausted; repeat the process a second time, and cork it down close in bottles.

The Housekeeper's Receipt Book, 1813

ROSE PERFUME

Take two pecks of fresh, dry damask rose-leaves; strip them from their leaves and stalks; have ready 16 pounds of fine hair-powder. Strew a layer of rose-leaves, on sheets of paper, at the bottom of a box, cover them over with a layer of hair-powder; then strew alternately a layer of roses and powder, until the whole of each has been used.

When they have lain 24 hours, sift the powder out, and expose it to the air 24 hours more. Stir it often. Add fresh rose-leaves, twice, as before, and proceed in the same way; after this dry the powder well by a gentle heat, and pass it through a fine sieve. Lastly, pour ten drops of oil of rhodium, or three drops of otto of roses, on loaf-sugar, which triturate in a glass mortar, and stir well into the powder, which put into a box, or glass, for use. This hair-powder perfume will be excellent, and will keep well.

Samuel and Sarah Adams, *The Complete Servant*, 1825

ROSE WATER

When the roses are full blown, pick off the leaves carefully, and allow a peck of them to a quart of water. Put them in a cold still over a slow fire, and distil it very gradually; bottle the water, and cork it up in two or three days.

The Housekeeper's Receipt Book, 1813

TO DRY HERBS

Sage and other herbs I have found keep best in powder, after they have been dried in an oven. Every leaf should be pulled off separately into a kind of tray made of tin, and put into an oven when about the right heat for baking bread; as soon as the leaves are dry enough to rub into powder, they should be crushed, and then put into wide-mouthed bottles, which should be carefully corked.

Mrs Loudon, *The Lady's Country Companion*, 1845

POT POURRI

Put into a large China jar the following ingredients in layers, with bay-salt strewed between the layers, two pecks of damask roses, part in buds and part blown; violets, orange-flowers, and jasmine, a handful of each; orris-root sliced, benjamin and storax, two ounces of each; a quarter of an ounce of musk; a quarter of a pound of angelica-root sliced; a quart of the red parts of clove-gillyflowers; two handfuls of lavender flowers; half a handful of rosemary flowers; bay and laurel leaves, half a handful of each; three Seville oranges, stuck as full of cloves as possible, dried in a cool oven, and pounded; half a handful of knotted marjoram; and two handfuls of balm of Gilead dried. Cover all quite close. When the pot is uncovered, the perfume is very fine.

A New System of Domestic Cookery, 1860

FOR PREVENTING HYSTERICS

Carraway seeds, finely pounded, with a small proportion of ginger and salt, spread upon bread and butter, and eaten every day, especially early in the morning, and at night before going to bed, is a good remedy against hysterics.

The Housewife's Receipt-Book, 1837

ORIGINAL RECEIPT FOR HUNGARY WATER

The original receipt for preparing this invaluable lotion, is written in letters of gold in the handwriting of Elizabeth, Queen of Hungary.

Take of acque vitae, four times distilled, 3 parts, the tops and flowers of rosemary, 2 parts.

To be put together in a close-stopped vessel, and allowed to stand in a warm place, during fifty hours, then to be distilled in an alembic, and of this, once every week, 1 drachm to be taken in the morning, either in the food or drink, and every morning the face and the deceased limb to be washed with it.

Samuel and Sarah Adams, *The Complete Servant*, 1825

TO MAKE BARLEY-SUGAR

INGREDIENTS.– *To every lb. of sugar allow ¹/₂ pint of water, ¹/₂ the white of an egg.*

Mode.– Put the sugar into a well-tinned saucepan, with the water, and, when the former is dissolved, set it over a moderate fire, adding the well-beaten egg before the mixture gets warm, and stir it well together. When it boils, remove the scum as it rises, and keep it boiling until no more appears, and the syrup looks perfectly clear; then strain it through a fine sieve or muslin bag, and put it back into the saucepan. Boil it again like caramel, until it is brittle, when a little is dropped in a basin of cold water; it is then sufficiently boiled. Add a little lemon-juice and a few drops of essence of lemon, and let it stand for a minute or two. Have ready a marble slab or large dish, rubbed over with salad-oil; pour on it the sugar, and cut it into strips with a pair of scissors; these strips should then be twisted, and the barley-sugar stored away in a very dry place. It may be formed into lozenges or drops, by dropping the sugar in a very small quantity at a time on to the oiled slab or dish.

*Time.–*¹/₄ hour. *Average cost, 7d*

Sufficient for 5 or 6 sticks.

Mrs Isabella Beeton, *The Book of Household Management*, 1861

SALLY LUNS

Take two pounds of flour, and add half a pint of milk and half a pint of cream, with a bit of butter the size of a walnut; when a little warm, put to it three well-beaten yolks of eggs, three or four spoonfuls of well-purified yeast, and a little salt. Mix the whole together, and let it rise for an hour; then make it into cakes, and lay them on tins lightly rubbed over with a little butter. Let them stand on the hearth to rise for about twenty minutes, covered with a thin cloth, then bake them in a rather quick oven.

Mrs Loudon, *The Lady's Country Companion*, 1845

TO FROST HOLLY-LEAVES, FOR GARNISHING AND DECORATING DESSERT AND SUPPER DISHES

INGREDIENTS.– *Sprigs of holly, oiled butter, coarsely-powdered sugar.*
Mode.– Procure some nice sprigs of holly; pick the leaves from the stalks, and wipe them with a clean cloth free from all moisture; then place them on a dish near the fire, to get thoroughly dry, but not too near to shrivel the leaves; dip them into oiled butter, sprinkle over them some coarsely-powdered sugar, and dry them before the fire. They should be kept in a dry place, as the least damp would spoil their appearance.

Time.– About 10 minutes to dry before the fire.

Seasonable.– These may be made at any time; but more suitable for winter garnishes, when fresh flowers are not easily obtained.

Mrs Isabella Beeton, *The Book of Household Management*, 1861

MUFFINS

Mix a pint and a half of warm milk and water, with a quarter of a pint of good yeast, and a little salt; stir them together for a quarter of an hour, then strain the liquor into a quarter of a peck of fine flour; mix the dough well and set it to rise for an hour, then roll it up and pull it into small pieces, make them up in the hand like balls, and lay a flannel over them while rolling to keep them warm. The dough should be closely covered up the whole time; when the whole is rolled into balls, the first that are made will be ready for baking. When they are spread out in the right form for muffins, lay them on tins and bake them, and as the bottoms begin to change colour turn them on the other side.

Samuel and Sarah Adams, *The Complete Servant*, 1825

QUINCE MARMALADE

Take quinces that are quite ripe, pare and cut them in quarters, take out the cores, put them in a stew-pan with spring water, nearly enough to cover them, keep them closely covered, and let them stew gently till they are quite soft and red, then mash and rub them through a hair sieve. Put them in a pan over a gentle fire, with as much thick clarified sugar as the weight of the quinces; boil them an hour and stir the whole time with a wooden spoon to prevent its sticking; put into pots, and when cold tie them down.

Samuel and Sarah Adams, *The Complete Servant*, 1825

TO CHOOSE EGGS AT MARKET

Put the large end of the egg to your tongue; if it feels warm it is new. In new-laid eggs, there is a small division of the skin from the shell, which is filled with air, and is perceptible to the eye at the end. On looking through them against the sun or a candle, if fresh, eggs will be pretty clear. If they shake they are not fresh.

A New System of Domestic Cookery, 1860

RATAFIA

Blanch two ounces of peach and apricot-kernels, bruise and put them into a bottle, and fill nearly up with brandy. Dissolve half a pound of white sugar-candy in a cup of cold water, and add the brandy after it has stood a month on the kernels, and they are strained off; then filter through paper, and bottle for use. The leaves of peach and nectarines, when the trees are cut in the spring, being distilled, are an excellent substitute for ratafia in puddings.

A New System of Domestic Cookery, 1860

TEA- AND COFFEE-POTS

When putting away the silver tea- and coffee-pot which is not used every day, lay a little stick across the top under the cover. This will allow the fresh air to get in, and prevent mustiness.

Things a Woman Wants to Know

A CURE FOR EARACHE

Procure an ordinary clay pipe, and insert a wad of cottonwool in the bowl, then drop six or eight minims of chloroform on to the wool, and cover with a similar wad. Insert the pipe stem just within the ear passage, and gently blow down the bowl of the pipe.

Domestic Life, 1897

FOR CHILBLAINS

Soak them in warm bran and water; then rub them well with mustard-seed flour. This must be done before they break.

The Housewife's Receipt-Book, 1837

CANDIED GINGER

Put 1 ounce of race ginger grated fine, a pound of loaf sugar beat fine, into a preserving pan, with as much water as will dissolve the sugar. Stir them well together over a slow fire till the sugar begins to boil. Then stir in another pound of sugar, beat fine, and keep stirring it till it grows thick. Then take it off the fire, and drop it in cakes upon earthen dishes. Set them in a warm place to dry, when they will become hard and brittle, and look white.

Samuel and Sarah Adams, *The Complete Servant*, 1825

FOR THE RELIEF OF PAIN

A simple and effective means of relieving pain, when suffering from neuralgia, is to apply a small bag of salt to the affected part. The salt should have been heated in the oven; it will retain the heat for a long time and give considerable relief.

The Servants' Own Paper, 1893

TO PREVENT FLIES FROM INJURING PICTURE-FRAMES, GLASSES, &C.

Boil three or four leeks in a pint of water, then with a gilding brush, do over your glasses and frames, and the flies will not go near the article so washed. This may be used without apprehension, as it will not do the least injury to the frames.

The Housewife's Receipt-Book, 1837

TO MAKE BARLEY-WATER

INGREDIENTS.– *2 oz. of pearl barley, 2 quarts of boiling water, 1 pint of cold water.*

Mode.– Wash the barley in cold water; put it into a saucepan with the above proportion of cold water, and when it has boiled for about 1/4 hour, strain off the water, and add the 2 quarts of fresh boiling water. Boil it until the liquid is reduced one half; strain it, and it will be ready for use. It may be flavoured with lemon-peel, after being sweetened, or a small piece may be simmered with the barley. When the invalid may take it, a little lemon-juice gives this pleasant drink in illness a very nice flavour.

Time.– To boil until the liquid is reduced one half.

Sufficient to make 1 quart of barley-water.

Mrs Isabella Beeton, *The Book of Household Management*, 1861

PICKLED OYSTERS

Wash four dozen large oysters in their own liquor, wipe them dry, strain off the liquor, add to it a spoonful of pepper, one of salt, three of white wine, four of vinegar, and two blades of mace. Simmer the oysters a few minutes in the liquor, put them into a small jar, boil up the pickles, and take off the scum. When cold, pour it over the oysters, and tie them down close.

The Housekeeper's Receipt Book, 1813

RICE-WATER

Wash three ounces of rice in several waters, and then put it into a very clean stewpan with a quart of water and an ounce of raisins; boil gently for half an hour, strain through a coarse hair sieve into a jug, and when cold, drink plentifully.

C. E. Francatelli, *The Cook's Guide and Housekeeper's and Butler's Assistant*, 1877

GREEN GOOSEBERRY WINE

Green Gooseberry Wine is made in the first manner, by crushing the fruit in a deep tub with a fruit-crusher, and then pouring cold water on it, in the proportion of one gallon of water to ten pounds of fruit. It is then left to stand about six hours, when the mass, or marc, as it is called, is put into a coarse bag and pressed; more water is then poured over the marc, which is again pressed, till as much water has been added as will make the proportion in all four gallons of water to ten pounds of fruit. The marc is then throw away, and to every gallon of the liquor, or must, as it is called, three pounds of lump sugar are added, and the whole is well stirred together; the tub is afterwards covered with a blanket, and the wine is left to ferment in a temperature of 55° to 60°. In twelve hours if the fermentation has begun rapidly, or in twenty-four hours if it is slow, the liquor is put into a cask and left to ferment, the bung being put in loosely, and the cask being kept filled up with fresh must as it works off. When the hissing noise subsides, the bung is driven in firmly, and a little hole is made in the head of the cask, near the bung, which is stopped with a wooden peg. In two or three days this peg is loosened to let any air out that may have been generated; and this is repeated, at intervals, several times, till no more air escapes, when the peg is driven in tight. An excellent wine may be made of the giant tart rhubarb, treated in this manner.

Mrs Loudon, *The Lady's Country Companion*, 1845

PICKLED WALNUTS

Gather them before the shells begin to form, pick off the stalks, and put them into a jar. Boil some good vinegar with a little salt and horseradish, some bruised pepper, ginger, and cloves, and pour it hot upon the bladder, and let them stand a year. When the walnuts are all used, the vinegar may be improved and made useful for fish sauce and hashes, by boiling it up with anchovies, cloves, and garlic: then strain it, and cork it up in bottles.

The Housekeeper's Receipt Book, 1813

ICES

The aged, the delicate, and children should abstain from ices or iced beverages; even the strong and healthy should partake of them in moderation. They should be taken immediately after the repast, or some hours after, because the taking of these substances *during* the process of digestion is apt to provoke indisposition. It is necessary, then, that this function should have scarcely commenced, or that it should be completely finished, before partaking of ices. It is also necessary to abstain from them when persons are very warm, or immediately after taking violent exercise, as in some cases they have produced illnesses which have ended fatally.

Mrs Isabella Beeton, *The Book of Household Management*, 1861

TO PRESERVE GRAPES

There are many ways of preserving grapes; but the best way is, to gather them with about five or six inches of the branch to each bunch, to seal the end with common sealiung wax, and to hang them to lines in a dry room. Examine them frequently, and cut out the mouldy berries.

Anne Cobbett, *The English Housekeeper*, 1842

TO PRESERVE PARSLEY THROUGH THE WINTER

Use freshly-gathered parsley for keeping, and wash it perfectly free from grit and dirt; put it into boiling water which has been slightly salted and well skimmed, and then let it boil for 2 or 3 minutes; take it out, let it drain, and lay it on a sieve in front of the fire, when it should be dried as expeditiously as possible. Store it away in a very dry place in bottles, and when wanted for use, pour over it a little warm water, and let it stand for about 5 minutes.

Seasonable.– This may be done at any time between June and October.

Mrs Isabella Beeton, *The Book of Household Management*, 1861

MUSHROOM KETCHUP

Break some large mushrooms, throw over them a good quantity of salt, and let them stand two nights. Strain and press out the liquor, and put it into a stewpan with black pepper bruised, sliced ginger, shalots, and horse-radish. Boil it an hour, strain it, and bottle it up quite close when it is cold. If well boiled, tied down properly, and set in a dry place, it will keep two or three years; otherwise it will soon spoil.

The Housekeeper's Receipt Book, 1813

TO CLARIFY ISINGLASS

Break your isinglass into small pieces with a hammer, wash it in several waters, and to four ounces add six pints of water; reduce it one-third, skimming it carefully; take it from the fire, and strain it through a silk sieve.

G. A. Jarrin, *The Italian Confectioner*, 1827

TO CLARIFY SUGAR

Break the white of an egg into a preserving pan; put to it 4 quarts of water, and beat it with a whisk to a froth. Then put in 12 pounds of sugar, mix all together, and set it over the fire. When it boils put in a little cold water, and proceed as often as necessary, till the scum rises thick on the top. Then remove it from the fire, and when it is settled, take off the scum, and pass it through a straining bag. If the sugar should not appear very fine, boil it again before straining it.

Samuel and Sarah Adams, *The Complete Servant*, 1825

TO MAKE LABELS STICK TO TIN

Add a little honey to common flour paste.

Things a Woman Wants to Know

TO FROST A WINDOW

Make a clear solution of gum arabic, dissolve some Epsom salts in hot water to make a very strong solution and add to it the gum arabic. Apply the mixture to the glass with a soft brush.

Things a Woman Wants to Know

TO APPLY LEECHES

The leeches should be kept out of the water for half an hour before applying them, and the skin whereon they are to be placed well washed and rubbed dry. A little sweetened milk smeared on the part will make them bite, and in placing them on the patient put the mouth, which is in the tapering end of its body, against the patient. Place them in a glass and turn it over on to the spot where it is wished they should bite. They must not be pulled off; when they have done their work they will come off; and they can be put into a plate of salt to make them vomit the blood. The leech-bites should be bathed with cold water till the bleeding stops, and then pads of lint applied. Never put leeches over a vein.

Mrs de Salis, *Wrinkles and Notions for Every Household*, 1890

TO PREVENT THE CREAKING OF A DOOR

Rub a bit of soap on the hinges.

A New System of Domestic Cookery, 1860

A CURE FOR THE STING OF WASPS OR BEES

A bruised leaf of the poppy, applied to the part affected, will give immediate relief.

C. E. Francatelli, *The Cook's Guide and Housekeeper's and Butler's Assistant*, 1877

BEECH BEDS

Beech beds are very springy to lie on, and the slight scent of the well-dried leaf is very pleasant. The leaves should be gathered on a dry day, and when put into the beds, well baked in a baker's oven. This kind of filling for a bed has a great advantage over others, for it will not harbour insects or vermin.

Things a Woman Wants to Know

TO RESTORE BROWN HOLLAND CHAIR COVERS

After they have been washed in the usual manner, they should be placed in water in which some hay has been boiled. This will restore the colour which has been washed out, and give them the appearance of new. It is also good for brown linen crumb cloths, and the covering of stair-carpets.

The Housekeeper, 1876

COMPOSITION FOR COVERING THE CORKS OF THE BOTTLES

May be easily purchased, or made in the following manner: melt a quantity of rosin, a fourth part of this quantity of bees' wax, and a fourth of brick-dust, and mix them well in a pot on the fire; dip the cork and the top of the bottle in it, turning it round, that it may completely cover the cork.

G. A. Jarrin, *The Italian Confectioner*, 1827

TO DESTROY FLIES

Ground black pepper and moist sugar, intimately mixed in equal quantities, and diluted with milk, placed in saucers, adding fresh milk and stirring the mixture as often as necessary, succeeds admirably in occasioning their death.

The Housewife's Receipt-Book, 1837

HARTSHORN JELLY

Use half a pound of hartshorn shavings, boil in three quarts of water, and reduce to one.

Alexis Soyer, *The Modern Housewife*, 1851

CURTAIN RINGS

Curtain rings sometimes run with great difficulty and seem to stick to the pole. To remedy this take all the rings off and well rub the pole with paraffin until it is quite smooth, when the rings may be replaced, and will be found to slip along with the greatest ease.

Things a Woman Wants

WASHING TABLE LINEN

When washing table linen, or any cloth stained with egg, avoid putting it in boiling water, which will set the stain till it is almost permanent. Soak the cloth first in cold water, and the stain may be easily removed. The same rule applies to egg-cups and any dishes stained with egg. If they are thrown with the other china, into hot soda-water, the stain hardens on the plate or glass, and it requires considerable patience to remove it; but it comes off easily in cold water.

Things a Woman Wants to Know

TO CLEAN FLAT IRONS

As is the brightness of the surface of a flat iron so will be the polish or finish of the article to be ironed. The irons should, therefore, be scrupulously clean and smooth; this can best be done by rubbing them with bees' wax and salt, and powdered bath brick. The heavier the iron the better the work. They should be used with a backward motion and heavy pressure.

The Servants' Own Paper, 1893

SCORCHES

Scorches made by overheated flat irons can be removed from linen, by spreading over the cloth a paste made of the juice pressed from two onions, $1/2$ oz. white soap, 2 ozs. fuller's earth, and $1/2$ pint vinegar. Mix, boil well, and cool before using.

The Housekeeper, 1876

TO WASH MUSLINS AND CHINTZES

Muslins and chintzes should always be treated agreeably to the oriental manner; that is, to wash them in plain water, and then boil them in *conjee*, or rice water; after which they ought not to be submitted to the operation of the smoothing iron, but rubbed smooth with a polished stone.

A New System of Practical Domestic Economy, 1842

BLUE

Blue is made by mixing and moulding indigo and Prussian blue into cakes of the required size. If any garments have been lying by for some time, and have become yellow, the best way to bleach them is to wash them in the ordinary way, rinse in blue-water, and then dry them in the open air, having repeated the rinsing and drying several times. If possible, they should be spread on a grass-plat in the sun.

Rev. J. P. Faunthorpe (ed.), *Household Science; Readings in Necessary Knowledge for Girls and Young Women*, 1881

FRENCH METHOD OF TAKING SPOTS OF INK OUT OF LINEN

Take a piece of mould candle, (or common candle will do nearly as well,) melt it, and dip the spotted part of the linen into the melted tallow. It may then be washed, or sent afterwards to the laundress, and the spots will be washed clean away, without injuring the linen. This is the best method hitherto discovered.

The School of Arts; or, Fountain of Knowledge

TO PERFUME LINEN

Rose leaves dried in the shade, cloves beat to a powder, and mace scraped; mix them together, and put the composition into little bags.

The Housewife's Receipt-Book, 1837

The Lady's Maid

The lady's maid, like the valet, needed a cheerful and sympathetic disposition and, most important of all, patience. Her business was to dress, change and undress her lady, to take care of her wardrobe and to make up cosmetic potions. She offered solicitude in indispositions (real and imaginary) and read to her mistress when she was too weak or idle for any other diversion. It was in her interest to study her mistress's temper and be sensitive and tolerant of changes in mood.

The author of *The Servants' Practical Guide* recognized several types of lady's maid: 'fine maids and humble maids, clever maids, and maids without any pretensions to cleverness; maids who are their mistress's "right hand" as it were, coadjutors in all that concerns the interest of the household; and maids who are mere automatons, who perform the duties required of them in a mechanical manner, and who are more alive to their own interests than that of their mistress; maids who act as housekeeper, and maids who act as nurse, first-class maids and second-class maids, experienced maids and inexperienced maids, smart maids and maids who are not smart; French maids and English maids'.

Swiss maids were competent and accommodating, but the best class of maid, it was agreed, was French. She was regarded as the best company and possessed of the greatest wit, but she was extravagant and haughty and suited, therefore, only for a wealthy household. She was 'only in her element in a large establishment, and households arranged on an economical footing did not meet the views of this order of lady's-maid; when engaged by the mistress of such, their stay with her is of the briefest, and too often fraught with annoyances and disagreeables to the household in general'. Provided the situation was to her liking, she was invaluable in making and

trimming dresses in the best taste and dressing hair in the most up-to-date Parisian manner.

Whatever her nationality, the lady's maid ranked as an upper servant and, in recognition of her position, was usually accorded a room to herself, in some houses with superior furnishings and her own maid. To avoid irritation to her mistress, she was advised to speak proper English, substituting 'a headache' for a 'sore head' and a refined 'come hither' (when addressing her lady's dog) for 'come here'. A pleasing accent was important when reading aloud.

Pretty manners and an agreeable appearance were important, too, in a servant in whose company a lady spent several hours of her day. Young lady's maids were preferred to old ones, and the scale of wages was apt to decrease in inverse proportion to age. Some middle-aged maids were promoted to housekeeper, but their lack of experience in cooking and ordering provisions was a disadvantage. If she were English, the lady's maid would probably have started in service as a housemaid, or as a dressmaker's assistant, in which case her skills would be particularly useful.

The principal perquisite of the lady's maid was cast-off finery. On her mistress's death she expected to receive her entire wardrobe, with the exception of articles specifically bequeathed elsewhere in her will. If arrangements existed for the clothes to be given away to poor relations when they were no longer wanted, the maid was told of this at the time of her engagement and higher wages were given in consequence. The clothes could be sold, but among the younger maids the temptation to wear them on duty, and especially on their days off, was hard to resist. This was frowned on – and she was warned in *The Duties of a Lady's Maid* (1825), 'never to dress out of your station, nor attempt to rival the ladies of the family. This is of more importance for you to guard against than if you were in any other station as a servant; for your knowledge of stuffs, trimmings, and fashions, gives you the means of doing this more successfully than any other servant'.

Her other perquisite, which in some instances amounted almost to a bribe, was her entitlement to commissions from the drapers, haberdashers and milliners patronized by her mistress. Wanting for nothing in the way of accommodation and food, if she did not save her money – and servants' manuals contained long passages of advice on how to be thrifty – she would spend it on dresses and bonnets.

The most time-consuming of a lady's maid's duties was the care of her mistress's wardrobe. 'A waiting-maid, who wishes to make herself useful', wrote Mrs Beeton, 'will study the fashion-books with attention, so as to be able to aid her mistress's judgment in dressing, according to the prevailing fashion, with such modifications as her style of countenance requires. She will also, if she has her mistress's interest at heart, employ her spare time in repairing and making up dresses which have served one purpose, to serve another also; or turning many things, unfitted for her mistress to use, for the younger branches of the family. The lady's maid may thus render herself invaluable to her mistress, and increase her own happiness in so doing. The exigencies of fashion and luxury are such, that all ladies, except those of the very highest rank, will consider themselves fortunate in having about them a thoughtful person, capable of diverting their finery to a useful purpose.'

Ladies of the highest rank usually had their dresses made by a dressmaker. The less well off had one or two from a dressmaker and the rest made at home by her maid. Mending, washing and cleaning were the maid's responsibility, and it was essential for her to know how to deal with stain from wax, fruit and ink on a variety of different stuffs. *The Complete Servant* gave separate instructions for cleaning black and white sarcenets (soft silk fabrics), washing and staining tiffanies (transparent gauze muslins), washing and starching lawns and cleaning white veils and black veils. She would have to know how to make velvet and crêpe look as good as new, how to clean feathers, silk and ribbons and revive artificial flowers, how to wash fine lace and linen, to dye gloves to various hues and to restore whiteness to scorched linen, perhaps using Mrs Beeton's method involving vinegar, fuller's earth, dried fowls' dung, soap and onion juice.

One 'wrinkle' that might have been passed on to her (or that she could have learned from a book such as *The Servants' Guide*) was: 'To counteract the unpleasant smell of clothes long laid-up in wardrobes, drawers &c., place newly-burnt charcoal among them, and the smell will cease in a day or two'. During the summer furs and woollen garments were put away with a piece of camphor or a tallow candle to protect them from the moth, and cedar shavings or shavings of Russia leather put in the drawers and shelves.

In helping her mistress to choose her dresses, the lady's maid had to have an eye for the effects of different colours on the complexion. 'If a colour appear beautiful in itself, that is not a sufficient reason why it should be made use of in a dress, or adopted by all women. Any colour whatever may be suited to certain persons, and be injurious to the beauty of many others. It is therefore necessary to choose not only the colour adopted by the tyranny of fashion, but that which best suits the complexion, and best harmonized with the other articles of dress with which it is intended to be worn'. This appeared in *The Duties of a Lady's Maid*, together with a description of the six different types of complexion: carnation, florid, fair, pale, sallow and brunette.

Under the title 'Colours in Dress', Samuel and Sarah Adams gave their views on the suitability of wearing clothes of a particular colour. 'Females of fair complexion ought to wear the purest white; they should choose light and brilliant colours, such as rose, azure, light yellow, &c. These colours heighten the lustre of their complexion, which if accompanied with darker colours, would frequently have the appearance of alabaster, without life and without expression'.

'On the contrary, women of a dark complexion, who dress in such colours as we too frequently see them do, cause their skin to appear black, dull, and tanned. They ought, therefore, to avoid wearing linen or laces of too brilliant a white; they ought to avoid white robes, and rose-colour, or light-blue ribbons, which form too disagreeable a contrast with their complexions'.

'Fair women cannot be too careful to correct, by light colours, the paleness of their complexions; and dark women, by stronger colours, the somewhat yellow tint of their complexion'.

'Crimson is extremely handsome at night, when it may be substituted for rose-colour, which loses its charms by candlelight; but this crimson, seen by day, spoils the most beautiful complexion; no colour whatever strips it so completely of all its attractions. Pale yellow, on the contrary, is often very handsome by day, and is perfectly suited to people who have a fine complexion; but at night it appears dirty, and tarnishes the lustre of the complexion, to which it is designed to add brilliancy'.

The Adams and other writers were of the opinion that summer veils should be green. White veils were thought to promote sunburn and freckles by increasing the power of the sun's light, and to be bad for the eyes.

The lady's maid's first duty in the morning was to call her mistress, having first made sure that the housemaid had swept and dusted the dressing-room and lit the fire. She laid out her clothes for the morning and brought up hot water for the basin or bath, which, before the days of plumbed in baths and bathrooms, was taken in front of the dressing-room fire. She was summoned by the bell to help her lady dress, lacing her corset and arranging the folds of her dress over the petticoats, then dressed her hair and assisted in the application of various tinctures and pomades to the skin and hair.

After breakfast she washed and removed stains from her mistress's dresses and linen, and then went to her own or the housekeeper's room, where she spent the rest of the morning ironing and sewing. If there were a still-room, she would help the housekeeper to concoct cures for afflictions such as the 'livid buttony pimple' and costiveness, lyes for washing and balms for wrinkles, freckles and sunburn and other defects of the complexion. Roman balsam made from bitter almonds, barley flour and honey, was recommended by the Adams as a cream to be worn at night and washed off in the morning, when other lotions were applied.

During the summer either the lady's maid or the housekeeper, sometimes with the assistance of a still-room maid, distilled toilet water and scented essences from garden plants – Hungary water, made from rosemary flowers, lavender and rose water, oil of jasmin and milk of roses.

Home-made lotions to keep the complexion smooth and white were most important to ladies at that time, as commercially available paints for the face often contained metallic oxides which were positively harmful to the complexion. White paint was especially pernicious and was known to cause inflammation of the skin and eyes and in some instances permanent injury to the face. The 'gentle Philander who may be anxious to ascertain whether his fair one's lilies and roses are really her own or not' was offered some advice in *A New System of Practical Domestic Economy*. 'Let him persuade her to take a trip to Harrogate, the waters of which fashionable place of resort are strongly impregnated with hydrogen, a gas that acts powerfully upon all the metallic oxides. When safely arrived at this new lecture room of nature, he may then try whether the bloom and brilliancy that withstood the test of hot rooms in Grosvenor-square, or Argyll-street, will likewise stand the test of those genial springs. If the fair one's face retains its pristine beauty after half a dozen ablutions, he may consider the article as genuine and unadulterated, and free from all the terrors of "Death in the Pot" – but if the dame or damsel begin to look blue, or turn black, he will at once perceive that beauty, like London porter, may be doctored for the market.'

Rouge, which was made from vegetable matter such as sandalwood, carmine obtained from cochineal or alkanet root mixed with talc or oil, was harmless by comparison with the mineral-based preparations, and so was rubbing the eyelashes and eyebrows with elderberries to blacken them.

In the afternoon or evening, depending on the hour appointed for dinner, the lady's maid helped her mistress dress. After the preparations for dinner came a long wait with little more to do than lay out her night clothes and attend to the bedroom and dressing-room fires until the bell rang for her to help her mistress undress for bed. She might have to wait up until three or four in the morning to untie a sash, unlace a corset, put away her lady's jewellery and remove the slops.

It was not unusual for the lady's maid to accompany her mistress when she paid visits to her friends. She packed the trunks, first laying out the clothes on the bed and chairs for her mistress to approve and then folding the dresses in calico wrappers. With her went the dressing-case, complete with looking-glass, brushes, boxes of pins and pots for cosmetics, and her work-box. She travelled in the carriage with her mistress, or in a different compartment in a railway train. On arrival, she unpacked and took care of her clothes as at home. Her meals were taken in the housekeeper's room, where, like the valet, she was warned to refrain from loose talk about her mistress and to converse on the subject of her position with discretion.

She was entrusted with confidences by her mistress, and what she was not told she often perceived. A faithful confidante was a luxury of the great lady, a loyal attendant who pandered to her every whim and protected her from unwelcome callers. The lady's maid was warned in particular to 'Have neither eyes, ears, nor understanding for what your mistress tries to conceal from you; there is nothing will sooner make you feared, distrusted, and ruined' *(The Duties of a Lady's Maid)*.

The Lady's Maid's Instructions and Receipts

HOW TO BLACKEN EYE-LASHES AND EYEBROWS

Rub them often with elder-berries. For the same purpose, some make use of burnt cork, or clove burnt at the candle.

The Duties of a Lady's Maid, 1825

ECONOMICAL ROUGE

Fine carmine, properly pulverized and prepared for the purpose, is the best that can be employed with safety and effect: it gives the most natural tone to the complexion, and imparts a brilliancy to the eyes, without detracting from the softness of the skin. To use it economically, take some of the finest pomatum, without scent, in which there is a proportion of white wax, about the size of a pea, just flatten it upon a piece of white paper, then take on a pointed penknife, carmine equal to a pin's head, mix it gently with the pomatum, with your finger, and when you have produced the desired tint, rub it in a little compressed cotton, pass it over the cheeks until colour is clearly diffused, void of grease. Ladies will find, upon trial, that this economical rouge will neither injure the health nor the skin; and it imitates perfectly the natural colour of the complexion.

Samuel and Sarah Adams, *The Complete Servant*, 1825

POMADE FOR REMOVING WRINKLES

Take two ounces of the juice of onions, the same quantity of the white lily, the same of Narbonne honey, and an ounce of white wax; put the whole into a new earthen pipkin till the wax is melted; take the pipkin off the fire, and, in order to mix the whole well together, keep stirring it with a wooden spatula till it grows quite cold. You will then have an excellent ointment for removing wrinkles. It must be applied at night, on going to bed, and not wiped off till the morning.

Samuel and Sarah Adams, *The Complete Servant*, 1825

LADY CONYNGHAM'S LIP-HONEY

Take two ounces of fine honey, one ounce of purified wax, half an ounce of silver litharge, the same quantity of myrrh. Mix over a slow fire, and add milk of roses, Eau de Cologne, or any other perfume you may prefer, and keep it for use.

Samuel and Sarah Adams, *The Complete Servant*, 1825

COLD CREAM

Melt together 1 dr. of white wax, 1 of spermaceti with 2 oz. of olive oil. Add 2 oz. of rosewater and 1/2 oz. of orange-flower-water. Rub together till they are thoroughly incorporated and the mixture is the consistency of cream.

Mrs de Salis, *Wrinkles and Notions for Every Household*, 1890

EXCELLENT TOOTH-BRUSH

Procure two or three dozen of the fresh roots of marshmallows, and dry them carefully in the shade, so that they may not shrivel. They must be chosen about as thick as a cane, and cut to five or six inches long, then with a mallet bruise the ends of them very gently, for about half an inch down, in order to form a brush. Then take two ounces of dragon's blood, four ounces of highly rectified spirit, and half an ounce of fresh conserve of roses, and put them in a glazed pipkin or pan, to dissolve over a gentle fire. When dissolved, put in your prepared mallow-roots, stirring them to make them take the dye equally. Continue this till no moisture remains in the vessel, when the roots will be hard, dry, and fit for use. If you take care of them, they will last you a considerable time. When you use this tooth-brush, it may be dipped in the following:

WASH FOR THE TEETH AND GUMS

Take the juice of half a lemon, a spoonful of very rough claret or port wine, ten grains of sulphate of quinine, a few drops of Eau de Cologne, or oil of bergamot.

Mix, and keep in a well-stopped phial for use.

Samuel and Sarah Adams, *The Complete Servant*, 1825

LYE FOR STRENGTHENING THE HAIR

Take two handsful of the root of hemp, same quantity of the roots of a maiden vine, same quantity of the cores of soft cabbages.

Dry and burn them, and make a lye of the ashes. Before you wash the hair with this lye, it should be well rubbed with honey, and this method persisted in for three days at least.

Samuel and Sarah Adams, *The Complete Servant*, 1825

TO MAKE AN EXCELLENT SMELLING BOTTLE

Take an equal quantity of sal-ammoniac and unslaked lime, pound them separate, then mix and put them in a bottle to smell to. Before you put in the above, drop two or three drops of the essence of bergamot into the bottle, then cork it close. A drop or two of ether, added to the same, will greatly improve it.

James W. Laughton, *The General Receipt-Book, c.* 1845

DRAUGHT FOR BAD BREATH WITH COSTIVENESS

Take one dram of sulphate of magnesia, two drams of tincture of calumba, an ounce and a half of infusion of roses.

Make a draught, to be taken every morning or every other morning, an hour before breakfast, for at least a month.

Samuel and Sarah Adams, *The Complete Servant,* 1825

HOW TO WASH CORSETS

To wash corsets, take out the steels in front and sides, lay them on a flat surface, and with a small brush scrub thoroughly with a tepid lather of white castile soap. When quite clean, let cold water run on them by holding them under a running tap until the soap is rinsed off. Pull them lengthwise till they are straight and shapely, and let them dry in a cool place, pulling them again and again until perfectly dry. Do not iron.

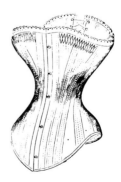

Domestic Life, 1897

TO CLEAN SILK STOCKINGS

Wash with soap and water; and simmer them in the same; put one drop of liquid blue, into a pan of cold spring water, run the stockings through this a minute or two, and dry them. For a pink cast, put one or two drops of saturates pink dye into cold water, and rinse them through this. For a flesh-colour, add a little rose-pink in a thin soap liquor, rub them with clean flannel, and calendar or mangle them.

Samuel and Sarah Adams, *The Complete Servant*, 1825

EXCELLENT PERFUME FOR GLOVES

Take of ambergris one drachm, civet the like quantity; add flour-butter a quarter of an ounce; and with these well mixed, rub the gloves over gently with fine cotton wool, and press the perfume into them.

Samuel and Sarah Adams, *The Complete Servant*, 1825

THE ART OF DYEING LEATHER GLOVES, RESEMBLING THE BEAUTIFUL YORK TAN, LIMERIC DYE, &C.

These pleasing hues of yellow, brown, or tan colour, are readily imparted to leather gloves by the following simple process: Steep saffron in boiling hot soft water for about twelve hours, then having slightly sewed up the top of the gloves, to prevent the dye from staining the insides, wet them over with a sponge or soft brush dipped into the liquor. The quantity of saffron, as well as of water, will of course depend on how much dye may be wanted; and their relative proportions, on the depth of colour required. A common tea cup will contain sufficient in quantity for a single pair of gloves.

The School of Arts; or, Fountain of Knowledge

TO CLEAN AND STARCH POINT LACE

Fix the lace in a prepared tent, draw it straight, make a warm lather of Castile soap, and, with a fine brush dipped in, rub over the point gently; and when it is clean on one side, do the same to the other; then throw some clean water on it, in which a little alum has been dissolved, to take off the suds, and having some thin starch, go over with the same on the wrong side, and iron it on the same side when dry, then open it with a bodkin, and set it in order.

Samuel and Sarah Adams, *The Complete Servant*, 1825

TO CLEAN WHITE SATIN AND FLOWERED SILKS

Mix sifted stale bread crumbs with powder-blue, and rub it thoroughly all over, then shake it well, and dust it with clean soft cloths. Afterwards, where there are any gold or silver flowers, take a piece of crimson in grain velvet, rub the flowers with it, which will restore them to their original lustre.

Samuel and Sarah Adams, *The Complete Servant*, 1825

TO CARE FOR PEARLS

As these will sometimes become discoloured, they may be readily restored to their original purity by a simple process. Soak them in hot water in which bran has been boiled with a little tartar and alum, rubbing them gently between the hands, when the heat will admit of it; when the water is cold, renew the application until the object is attained, when the pearls may be rinsed in luke-warm water, and laid on white paper in a convenient dark place to cool.

A New System of Practical Domestic Economy, 1824

WHITE CLOTHING

White clothing, if put away in a dark closet or drawer will become yellow. But if it is placed in a box lined with blue paper, or even wrapped in a dark blue cloth, it will come out as white as ever it was, no matter how long it lies. To whiten clothes that have become yellow, steep them overnight in lukewarm water, and next morning wash them in good, clean suds, then put them in a copper, with cold water, and some bits of curd soap, and one teaspoonful of powdered borax. Boil for twenty minutes, rinse immediately, and leave them for another night in clean cold water, to which a little powdered borax has been added.

Things a Woman Wants to Know

RINGS LOOSENED FROM THE FINGER

If a gold ring sticks tight on the finger, and cannot easily be removed, touch it with mercury, and it will become so brittle that a single blow will break it.

The Housekeeper's Receipt Book, 1813

TO CLEAN WHITE OSTRICH FEATHERS

Four ounces of white soap, cut small and dissolve in four pints of warm water; make the solution into a lather by beating. Introduce the feathers, and rub well with the hands for five or six minutes. After this soaping wash them in clean water, as hot as the hands can bear. Shake before the fire until dry.

Things a Woman Wants to Know

BUTTONS

Sew on buttons over a darning-needle, and when done pull out the needle. The buttons will be found much looser than those sewn on in the ordinary way, and will not pull off so easily.

Things a Woman Wants to Know

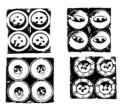

OIL OF JASMIN

Take an iron plate, on this place a cotton cloth, imbued with olive oil, then a layer of flowers, then a cloth, and lastly an iron plate; repeat the series as convenient, and change the flowers for fresh ones, until a proper scent is imparted; then apply pressure, collect the oil in glass bottles, and let it rest until fine; lastly, pour off the clear.

The Household Cyclopaedia, 1856

FRENCH METHOD OF WASHING FINE LACE OR LINEN

Take a gallon of furze-blossoms, and burn them to ashes, then boil them in six quarts of soft water; this when fine you may use in washing, with your suds, as occasion requires, and you will have the lace or linen, &c. not only exceeding white, but it may be done with half the soap, and little trouble.

The School of Arts; or, Fountain of Knowledge

HARD WATER

When unable to procure soft water for toilet purposes, keep a muslin bag with fine oatmeal in it, and squeeze out in water before washing. Put fresh oatmeal every day.

Things a Woman Wants to Know

TO CLEAN KID GLOVES

Take fifteen drops of strong solution of ammonia and half a pint of spirit of turpentine. Either put the gloves on your own hands or on wooden hands, and apply the mixture with a brush. Then rub the gloves with pumice-powder. Apply the mixture again, this time with a flannel. Repeat the process, two or three times, until clean, and then hang them in the air to dry, and to lose the smell of turpentine.

Things a Woman Wants to Know

HARD POMATUM

Take *30 pounds of suet.*
  1 1/2 pounds of white wax,
  6 ounces of essence of bergamot,
  4 ounces of lemon,
  1 oz. of lavender,
  4 drachms of oil of rosemary, and
  2 drachms of essence of ambergris.
Shred and pick the suet clean, and melt in an earthen pan or pipkin. Then stir it well and strain; and when nearly cold, add the perfumes, stirring well as before; when properly mixed, pour it into tin moulds.

Samuel and Sarah Adams, *The Complete Servant*, 1825

INFALLIBLE CORN-PLASTER

Take two ounces of gum ammoniac, two ounces of yellow wax, six drams of verdigris. Melt them together, and spread the composition on a bit of soft leather, or a piece of linen. Cut away as much of the corn as you can with a knife, before you apply the plaster, which must be renewed in a fortnight, if the corn is not by that time gone.

Samuel and Sarah Adams, *The Complete Servant*, 1825

PERFUMED BAGS FOR DRAWERS

Cut, slice, and mix well together, in the state of very gross powder, the following ingredients:

2 oz. of yellow saunders,
2 oz. of coriander seeds,
2 oz. of orris root,
2 oz. of calamus aromaticus,
2 oz. of cloves,
2 oz. of cinnamon bark
2 oz. of dried rose leaves,
2 oz. of lavender flowers, and
1 lb. of oak shavings.

When properly mixed, stuff the above into small linen bags, which place in drawers, wardrobes, &c., which are musty, or liable to become so.

Samuel and Sarah Adams, *The Complete Servant*, 1825

HOW TO PERFUME NOTEPAPER

Get a few quires of blotting-paper, and sprinkle each sheet with the perfume required, then put it under a weight until it becomes dry. When dry put the notepaper and envelopes between the sheets, and put them under a weight for a few hours. When removed they will be found perfumed. The blotting-paper sheets may be utilised several times, and can be made to retain their perfume for a long time by keeping them from exposure to the air.

Things a Woman Wants to Know

TO CLEAN SILK OR RIBBONS

INGREDIENTS. – *1/2 pint of gin, 1/2 lb. of honey, 1/2 lb. of soft soap, 1/2 pint of water.*

Mode.– Mix the above ingredients together; then lay each breadth of silk upon a clean kitchen table or dresser, and scrub it well on the soiled side with the mixture. Have ready three vessels of cold water; take each piece of silk at two corners, and dip it up and down in each vessel, but do not wring it; and take care that each breadth has one

vessel of quite clean water for the last dip. Hang it up dripping for a minute or two, then dab it in a cloth, and iron it quickly with a very hot iron.

Mrs Isabella Beeton, *The Book of Household Management*, 1861

TO RAISE THE SURFACE OF VELVET

Warm a smoothing iron moderately, and cover it with a wet cloth, and hold it under the velvet; the vapour arising from the heated cloth will raise the pile of the velvet with the assistance of a rush whisk.

The Housewife's Receipt-Book, 1837

TO TAKE OUT PITCH, WAX, ROSIN, OR TAR

If any of these happen on a garment, either silk, linen, or woollen, pour a little oil of turpentine on the place, and let it soak in about half an hour; then rub it, but not too hard, and you will find the turpentine has soaked out the glutinous qual-ity, so that it will crumble out like small bits of dry dirt.

The School of Arts; or, Fountain of Knowledge

The Housemaid

It is not possible to prevent dirt', wrote a contributor to *The Housekeeper* magazine in 1876, resigned to the truth, 'for as long as matter is divisible, dust, mud, and smuts will come'. It was the housemaid's job to prevent the accumulation of dirt, which not only disfigured the furniture and spoiled the look of the whole room, but 'soils the flesh and clothes of the persons who touch it and spreads disease', by a tedious routine of sweeping, dusting and scouring every corner of the house.

The housemaid was expected to rise between five and half-past six in the morning (just as the butler was slipping down to the cellar to taste and treat the wine) and accomplish many of her chores before the family was awake, for it was thought that the sight or sound of a housemaid, or of her equipment, would offend those of gentle birth.

An under housemaid began her day by opening the shutters and windows of the downstairs rooms. She moved all the small articles of furniture into the centre of the room and took up the hearth rug, which she carried outside to shake or beat, and then she removed the fender. Upholstered furniture and the piano, if there were one, she covered with dust sheets. Next, she was instructed to 'Strew moist tea-leaves over the carpet, and sweep with the carpet-broom; sweep steadily, but not with too much force; the more force you use, the more dust you will make. Having swept all round the room, replace the chairs, &c., and strew fresh tea-leaves over the middle of the room, and sweep as before. Sweep towards the door, or fireplace. Gather up the dust and take it away at once. Leave the room for a little while until the dust is settled' *(The Housekeeper)*. Sometimes salt or fresh grass were used to lay the dust instead of tea-leaves.

Next she laid a drugget in front of the fireplace and on it placed her housemaid's box, containing black lead, brushes, leathers and cloths, brickdust and emery paper, and the cinder pail, a bucket with a lid and wire sifter usually of japanned tin. The ashes were thrown away but the cinders were kept and used again for the fire or for the kitchen stove. The bars of the grate and the fire irons were rubbed with oil and afterwards with brickdust or emery paper to make them shine. The fender was polished in the same way. The backs and sides of the fireplace were blackleaded, or varnished with Brunswick black if the fire was not to be lit for a time, and the hearth scoured. Then she laid the fire or, at the beginning of the summer arranged a paper or other ornament in the grate, and occasionally cleaned the woodwork or marble of the fireplace. Finally, when the dust had settled, she dusted the room.

Old silk handkerchiefs were used as dusters, and paint brushes and feathers. Susanna Whatman, the wife of an eighteenth-century paper manufacturer and a punctilious housekeeper, recommended a goose's wing for dusting books. 'One of the most useful common directions next to carrying a candle upright', she wrote, 'is that of putting away chairs, tables and anything that goes next to a wall, with a hand behind it. For want of this trifling attention, great pieces are frequently knocked out of the stucco, and the backs of chairs, if bending, leave a mark on the wall'. Bellows were sometimes used to blow away the dust on gilded mirror and picture frames and on textiles, and special care had to be taken not to dislodge the pendants of glass chandeliers. Every object of brass, even to the bows of the door keys, were polished till they shone; the tops of worn-out woollen stockings sewn together made good polishing pads. From the dining-room or breakfast room and the drawing-room, the housemaid moved on to the other rooms on the ground floor, to the morning-room, parlour, sitting-room, study or library, according to the date, whereabouts and size of the house. Before tackling the entrance hall, she might stop for breakfast, eaten in the servants' hall or in the kitchen of a smaller establishment. Still to be done over before the family came down to breakfast were the front steps, front staircase and passages. Floorboards were scrubbed with fuller's earth and fine sand. By the late nineteenth century the entrance hall and passages of town houses often had oil cloth covering the boards, but stone and marble floors generally remained in the country.

In households where no lady's maid was kept, the housemaid – either the upper housemaid or, when the work was shared between two maids, the one responsible for the upper floor – was expected to lay out the mistress's clothes and prepare for her toilet just as the butler or footman might perform the duties of a valet. Before the lady was woken, the housemaid swept and dusted her dressing-room and lit the fire.

The drudgery of her job consisted mainly in carrying heavy buckets and cleaning utensils up the back stairs from the housemaid's cupboard and down again. Even in town houses where there was running water, it was often supplied only to the basement.

It was usual for the housemaids to make the beds in pairs; where only one was kept, she might be helped by the kitchen maid or even the cook in a small household. 'In bed-making, the fancy of its occupant should be consulted: some like beds sloping from the top towards the feet, swelling slightly in the middle; others, perfectly flat; a good housemaid will accommodate each bed to the taste of the sleeper, taking care to shake, beat, and turn it well in the process. Some persons prefer sleeping on the mattrass; in which case a feather bed is usually beneath resting on a second mattrass, and a straw palliasse at the bottom. In this case, the mattrasses should change places daily; the feather bed placed on the mattrass shaken, beaten, taken up and opened several times, so as thoroughly to separate the feathers; if too large to be thus handled, the maid should shake and beat one end first, and then the other, smoothing it afterwards equally all over into the required shape, and place the mattrass gently over it. Any feathers which escape in this process a tidy servant will put back through the seam of the tick' *(The Book of Household Management)*. Hair mattrasses were sometimes used in conjunction with straw palliasses, and the latter had to be remade at least once a year. According to the Adams, housemaids were supposed to wash their hands and put on a clean apron before making the beds.

The housemaid's duties in the bedroom included the search for – and extermination of – unwelcome inhabitants of the beds. 'As the

utmost attention to cleanliness will not always prevent the intrusion of certain little insects, too indelicate to name, but which take longer leaps in proportion to their size than any other known animal in existence, it has been customary to scatter fresh leaves of penny-royal in bed-chambers as an antidote against their appearance' *(A New System of Practical Economy)*. The Victorians favoured brass bedsteads (cast-iron ones for the servants) because wooden testers were thought to harbour these creatures in the joints and cracks.

The paper on top of the four-poster beds was to be changed twice a year, according to Susanna Whatman, and cleaning under the beds was done at least once a week. Special long-handled mops and brooms were made for the purpose, perhaps saving a few house-maids from the knee complaint with which their name is associated. Carpet sweepers became available in Britain after Bissell invented his machine known as the Grand Rapids sweeper in 1876.

Floorboards in the bedrooms were not to be scrubbed on wet or foggy days as the wood was slow to dry. In winter fires were lit so that the rooms would be dry by nightfall. The garret and servants' rooms were cleaned two or three times a week, but no such precautions against the damp were taken and in most of them there was no carpet to be brushed.

Once a year in the country and twice a year in large cities the carpets were taken up and the room 'turned out'. The carpets were sometimes washed with vinegar to restore their colours. The housemaids usually started at the top of the house and worked steadily downwards room by room. During the summer muslin curtains were often put up in place of the heavier winter ones.

For her morning's work the housemaid wore a simple cotton print dress and apron. A length of material was given to her at Christmas as her only present from the mistress of the house, and she made it up herself. From the 1860s onwards the print dress was exchanged in the afternoon for a black dress and white apron and cap, both becoming more elaborate towards the end of the century.

In the afternoons the housemaid busied herself with turning and mending the sheets and marking the household linen. In a properly run establishment each article was dated and numbered, and marked with the mistress's initials. Some afternoons, perhaps once a week, she might be required to help in the laundry with mangling and folding the table linen, sheets, pillowcases and bolster cases. All through the day there were blinds to be lowered in time to prevent the sunlight from damaging the contents of the rooms.

An hour or so before the family dressed for dinner, it was time to light the dressing-room fires. The bedroom fires were left until after dinner, when the beds were turned down and in winter warming pans or water bottles put in them. The readers of *A New System of Domestic Economy* were cautioned 'against the use of charcoal in warming pans, or even of common coals, until they have burnt to a cinder. To the healthy, the vapours thence arising and left in the bed, where they remain on account of their destiny, are often troublesome; but to the sick, they are palpably injurious, and frequently prompt to that cough which annoys the phthisicky and asthmatic, the moment they lie down for repose. Where circumstances require a bed to be heated at a moment's notice, a little salt thrown into the warming pan, and suffered to burn for a minute previous to use, will generally be beneficial; and as chambermaids are seldom either philosophers or chemists, it may be better to make this a standing order than to trust to their judgment on gaseous combustion.'

When there was company the housemaid was expected to help wash the dishes in the pantry and, in the absence of a still-room maid, an under housemaid waited at table in the housekeeper's room. In the evenings she did her own washing and sewing. Worn out by climbing the back stairs, discouraged by the monotony of her work and the lack of contact with the people she served, and without the first-hand view of their lives on which some of the other servants thrived, she probably went early to her bed. This she might share with another servant-girl, and, if she were very unlucky, with the leaping insects from which she was supposed to protect her superiors.

The Housemaid's Instructions and Receipts

CLEANING WOODWORK

Where painted wainscot or other wood-work requires cleansing, fuller's earth will be found cheap and useful: and, on wood not painted, it forms an excellent substitute for soap. Where extreme nicety is required, use a mixture of one pound of soft soap, two ounces of pearl-ash, one pint of sand and one pint of table-beer. Simmer these substances in a pipkin over a slow fire, and let them be well mixed. The mode of application is to put a small quantity in flannel, rubbing it on the wainscot; wash it off with warm water, and dry thoroughly with a linen cloth. Another method of cleaning white paint is by grating potatoes to a very fine pulp, in the proportion of four to every quart of water: the whole must be well stirred, and then suffered to settle, when the liquor may be poured off, and a sponge dipped in it for use.

A New System of Practical Domestic Economy, 1842

THE CARE OF BROOMS

If brooms are dipped once a week for a minute or two in a kettle of boiling suds they will last much longer. It makes them tough but pliable, and a carpet is not worn half so much by sweeping treated in this manner.

Things a Woman Wants to Know

TO DUST CARPETS AND FLOORS

Sprinkle tea-leaves, then sweep carefully. Carpets should not be swept frequently with a whisk brush, as it wears them very fast; about once a week is sufficient; at other times use tea-leaves and a hair brush. When you sweep a room, throw a little wet sand all over it, and that will gather up all the dust and flew, prevent it from rising, clean the boards, and save the bedding, pictures and other furniture from dust or dirt.

The Housewife's Receipt-Book, 1837

TO RENOVATE GREEN BLINDS

To make faded green blinds look like new, brush them well, and then lightly brush over with linseed oil.

Things a Woman Wants to Know

TO CLEAN PAPER HANGINGS

First blow off the dust with the bellows. Divide a white loaf of eight days old into eight parts. Take the crust into your hand, and beginning at the top of the paper, wipe it downwards in the lightest manner with the crumb. Don't cross nor go upwards. The dirt of the paper and the crumbs will fall together. Observe, you must not wipe above half a yard at a stroke, and after doing all the upper part, go round again, beginning a little above where you left off. If you don't do it extremely light, you will make the dirt adhere to the paper. It will look like new if properly done.

A New System of Domestic Cookery, 1860

TO CLEAN BOARDS, AND GIVE THEM A VERY NICE APPEARANCE

After washing them well with soda and warm water and a brush, wash them with a vary large sponge and clean water. Both times, observe to leave no spots untouched; – clean straight up and down, not crossing from board to board; dry with clean cloths, rubbing hard up and down in the same way. Floors should not often be wetted, but very thoroughly when done; and once a week dry-rubbed with hot sand, and a heavy brush the right way of the boards. The sides of stairs or passages, on which are carpets or floor cloth, should be washed with sponge instead of flannel or linen, and the edges will not be soiled. Different sponges should be kept for the above uses; and those and the brushes should be washed clean when done with, and kept in a dry place.

The Housewife's Receipt-Book, 1837

HOW TO CLEAN STONE STAIRS

Boil one quart of water with one cake of pipeclay, one table-spoonful of carbonate of lime, three ounces of size, and half the quantity of stone blue. Boil well together, and when cold, use. Wash the stairs with plenty of clean cold water, wipe them dry, and then rub lightly with the mixture. When quite dry, rub the stones with a brush and flannel till the floors look well.

Things a Woman Wants to Know

STRAW MATTING

Straw matting will look bright and fresh at the end of summer if it is carefully washed over with a soft cloth wrung out of salt and water every time it is swept.

Things a Woman Wants to Know

POISON FOR BUGS

Spirits of wine, and spirits of turpentine, of each four ounces; white mercury and camphor, of each half an ounce: mix. A chemist will make it up; and it must be applied with a brush to the bedstead or box infested with the insects.

The Housekeeper, 1876

TO RESTORE THE MAHOGANY TOP OF A BATH

Wash thoroughly with warm water and soap, and when dry apply with a flannel the following polish and rub after with a soft dry cloth: Mix ½ pint brown vinegar, ¼ pint linseed oil, 1 wineglassful of spirits of wine. Shake the mixture well. If very shabby it will require several applications.

Mrs de Salis, *Wrinkles and Notions for Every Household*, 1890

REMEDIES AGAINST FLEAS

Fumigation with brimstone, or the fresh leaves of penny-royal sewed in a bag, and laid on a bed, will have the desired effect.

The School of Arts; or, Fountain of Knowledge

DISHCLOTHS

Dishcloths may be knitted on coarse wooden needles of the string which is tied round tradesmen's parcels. They are strong and have a rough surface, and are capital for cleaning. They should be boiled in soda-water to keep them sweet.

Things a Woman Wants to Know

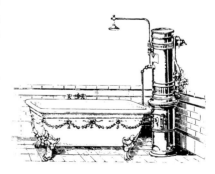

TO CLEAN BATHS

When a scum forms on the inside of the bath, or the stationary marble wash-basins, rub the places with dry salt, and they will come off without any trouble.

Things a Woman Wants to Know

POLISH FOR BRIGHT STOVES AND STEEL ARTICLES

INGREDIENTS.– *1 tablespoonful of turpentine, 1 ditto of sweet oil, emery powder.*

Mode.– Mix the turpentine and sweet oil together, stirring in sufficient emery powder to make the mixture of the thickness of cream. Put it on the article with a piece of soft flannel, rub off quickly with another piece, then polish with a little dry emery powder and clean leather.

Mrs Isabella Beeton, *The Book of Household Management*, 1861

BRUNSWICK BLACK FOR GRATES

INGREDIENTS.–*1 lb. of common asphaltum, ¹/₂ pint of linseed oil, 1 quart of oil of turpentine.*

Mode.– Melt the asphaltum, and add gradually to it the other two ingredients. Apply this with a small painter's brush, and leave it to become perfectly dry. The grate will need no other cleaning, but will merely require dusting every day, and occasionally brushing with a dry black-lead brush. This is, of course, when no fires are used. When they are required, the bars, cheeks, and back of the grate will need black-leading in the usual manner.

Mrs Isabella Beeton, *The Book of Household Management*, 1861

TO TREAT LEATHER

Leather that has become dull and shabby-looking may be very much improved in appearance by being rubbed over with the white of an egg well beaten.

Things a Woman Wants to Know

TO CLEAN ALL SORTS
OF METAL

Mix half a pint of refined neat's-foot oil, and half a gill of spirits of turpentine; wet a woollen rag therewith, dip it into a little scaped rotten-stone, and rub the metal well. Wipe it off with a soft cloth, polish with dry leather, and use more of the powder. If steel is very rusty, use a little powder of pumice with liquid, on a separate woollen rag, first.

Samuel and Sarah Adams, *The Complete Servant*, 1825

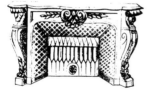

SUMMER ORNAMENTS
FOR GRATES

Purchase two yards and a half of crinoline muslin, and tear it into small strips, the selvage way of the material, about an inch wide; strip this thread by thread on each side, leaving the four centre threads; this gives about six-and-thirty pieces, fringed on each side, which are tied together at one end, and fastened to the trap of the register, while the threads, unravelled, are spread gracefully about the grate, the lower part of which is filled with paper shavings. This makes a very elegant and very cheap ornament, which is much stronger, besides, than those usually purchased.

Mrs Isabella Beeton, *The Book of Household Management*, 1861

TO BLACKEN THE FRONTS OF STONE
CHIMNEY-PIECES

Mix oil-varnish with lamp-black, and a little spirit of turpentine, to thin it to the consistence of paint. Wash the stone with soap and water very clean, then sponge it with clear water; and when perfectly dry, brush it over twice with this colour, letting it dry between the times. It looks extremely well. The lamp-black must be sifted first.

A New System of Domestic Cookery, 1860

The Cook and Kitchen Maids

Cook Wanted – a respectable middle-aged person, of strict integrity and cleanly industrious habits, who well understands making bread, pastry, soups, &c. her business generally, and management with care and economy. Persons accustomed to the country preferred. No perquisites allowed. An unexceptionable character required', reads an advertisement in *The Times* for 21 April 1847. On the back page of the newspaper cooks of all sorts, 'good plain cooks', 'plain cooks', cooks who acted as housekeepers, and 'professed' cooks, described their skills and preferences and offered their services to employers. Some specified a position in a nobleman's family, others sought work in a household where a footman was kept or more than one kitchen maid.

'The duties of a cook', wrote the author of *The Servants' Practical Guide* of 1880, 'depend greatly upon the scale of establishments to which she belongs. In the case of a professed cook, the elementary portion of the cooking, the plain cooking, and all that relates to cleaning and scouring in kitchen, scullery, larder, and passages, and all cooking utensils, is done by the kitchen and scullery maids, and only the cooking proper is the duty of this class of cook. All ingredients are prepared for her use, and the kitchen-maids wait upon her and act under her orders'.

A plain cook in a small household had no assistants and was expected to perform duties unconnected with the cooking such as sweeping and dusting the dining-room and answering the door in the morning while the housemaid was busy cleaning upstairs. She was often self-taught rather than trained by a professed cook in a large household, and was not able to prepare complicated dishes or arrange menus.

A male cook, or chef, was thought superior to a female professed cook. In the eighteenth century he was traditionally French, sometimes presiding over female under cooks; but an Englishman trained in France was acceptable in some households. Monsieur Menager, Royal Chef to Queen Victoria, had his own London house and arrived in the morning by hansom. In the 1890s, when an apprentice cook earned £15 a year, Monsieur Menager was paid the magnificent sum of £500. Working beneath him were master chefs, each of whom took charge of a particular dish, presenting it to him at different stages of its creation for his approval.

Queen Victoria also employed an Italian confectioner, and Indian cooks for the curries that were prepared each day after she became Empress of India, but by 1869 it was said in a new edition of Mrs Beeton that 'It is in the large establishments of princes, noblemen, and very affluent families alone, that the man-cook is found in this country'.

The superior the cook, the less the mistress of the house was consulted about the menu. It was usual, however, for a professed cook to make out on a slate the day's menus (sometimes for the servants' meals as well) and take them up to the mistress or send them up with a footman at about eleven o'clock. To judge by the nature of the advice frequently offered to young housewives, cooks were often difficult to deal with, unpredictable except in their unwillingness to accept reproof and readiness to give notice at the smallest pretext. Their standing in the household was acknowledged by their employers and the other servants by the use of the courtesy title 'Mrs', but Mrs Beeton, brisk as always, wrote: 'The kitchen must no longer be *sanctum sanctorum*, into which even the mistress cannot enter without being considered as an impertinent intruder, and liable to the sauciness of those whose grand secret is to become the domestic tyrants, in whatever comes within the scope of their management'.

The first culinary duty of the day was to make the dough for the household bread and breakfast rolls. Yeast brought from the local brewery was often bitter and required frequent washing in water that was changed each day. Alternatively, it could be made at home by fermenting split peas. The baking was generally done in a brick oven, even after the introduction of cast-iron ovens attached to the kitchen range. 'A brick oven should be well heated with faggot wood, or with a faggot, and two or three solid logs; and after it is cleared, the door should be closely shut for quite half an hour before the baking commences: the heat will then be well sustained for a succession of bread, pies, cakes, and small pastry', wrote Eliza Acton in *Modern Cookery for Private Families*, first published in 1845. 'The servant who habitually attends at an oven will soon become acquainted with the precise quantities of fuel which it requires, and all other peculiarities which may be connected with it'.

Until enclosed kitchen ranges with an oven on one side and a boiler for heating water on the other were installed – in most large houses in the first half of the nineteenth century – all the cooking except the baking was done over an open fire. Meat was roasted on a spit, once turned by a kitchen boy or a dog on a treadwheel; later inventions were the smoke jack, driven by currents of hot air from the fire, and the clockwork spit jack. To one side of the fireplace there was generally a warming cupboard set into the brickwork.

An economical method of roasting meat was on a hook suspended inside a screen with a brightly polished curved surface which reflected the heat from the fire. The hook was turned by means of a wheel and chain. Basting was done through a door in the back of the screen and the dripping fell into a pan beneath.

Improvements to stoves in the nineteenth century were paralleled by the invention of numerous ingenious containers and gadgets for cooking and preparing food. Cutlet and haricot cutters, paste jaggers, moulds in elaborate shapes for jellies and creams, graters and mincers were among the items illustrated in trade publications and cookery books of the mid-century.

Recipes, not so much intended to be followed by cooks as for the instruction of their middle-class employers, became increasingly economical in their ingredients and precise in their directions, a change initiated by Eliza Acton. 'It is a popular error', she wrote, 'to imagine that what is called good cookery is adapted only to the establishments of the wealthy, and that it is beyond the reach of those who are not affluent. On the contrary, it matters comparatively little whether some few dishes, amidst an abundant variety, be prepared in their perfection or not; but it is of the utmost consequence that the food which is served at the more simply supplied tables of the middle classes should all be well and skilfully prepared, particularly as it is from these classes that the men principally emanate to whose indefatigable industry, high intelligence, and active genius, we are mainly indebted for our advancement in science, in art, in literature, and in general civilisation'.

An important element in domestic economy and the production of wholesome palatable food was the careful supervision of the larders and store rooms. Salt meat and fish hung with the dried herbs from the kitchen rafters in small establishments, but in a large country house there would be a range of store rooms close to the kitchen, as well as separate rooms for baking, salting and smoking. The larder in a country house, advised Mrs Loudon in *The Lady's Country Companion*, 'is generally a square or oblong room near the kitchen, and sometimes sunk below it. It should be kept as cool as possible, and should be contrived to be on the north side of the house'. Free-standing game larders were often situated in the kitchen courtyard.

The meat was weighed when it was delivered to a town house to make sure that it corresponded with the order, and cooked meat was often locked in a meat safe to prevent pilfering by the servants. Dry stores were ordered and handed out by the housekeeper, but the cook was responsible for testing flour and spices for adulteration. The cook's perquisites – expressly forbidden in *The Times* advertisement – traditionally consisted of dripping from the roast and, since tea was an expensive commodity, tea leaves that could be re-brewed. These were sold to traders and to the poor who came to the back door.

In the country milk came from the dairy, which was sometimes attached to the house. The dairy maid, in this case, was a kitchen maid with particular duties. Ideally the dairy faced north, like the larder, and had a tiled floor and walls for reasons of coolness and hygiene. The milk was brought in twice a day in a can or wooden pail. It was strained and then poured into shallow milk pans while still warm from the cow to allow the cream to rise. The morning's milk was skimmed in the afternoon and the afternoon's the following morning. The cream was used at table, for cooking and for making butter. Most cheeses were made from unskimmed milk. The work of the dairy maid, including the scalding of wooden and earthenware vessels, was supervised by the cook.

The kitchen utensils were washed in soda and water and scoured by scullery maids, who also blacked and lit the kitchen range in the early morning, and cleaned the scullery, larders, kitchen passages and servants' hall. The 'slaveys', as they were called, did not use the servants' hall but ate in the kitchen with the kitchen maids.

The duties of the kitchen maids in a medium-sized household, according to *The Servants' Guide and Family Manual* of 1830, were 'to take nearly the whole management of roasting, boiling, and otherwise dressing all plain joints and dishes, and all the fish and vegetables. The cleanliness of the kitchen is likewise one of her foremost duties – as scouring the dressers, shelves, and kitchen-tables.' They prepared the vegetables, game, poultry and fish, took charge of the bread and pastry making, cooked for the nursery, schoolroom and servants' hall and worked in the dairy.

A chef or professed cook, with the preparation of ingredients and the elementary cooking delegated to the kitchen staff, was able to concentrate on the complicated dishes. These were principally the entrées: light dishes, which preceded the roasts, done up in a sauce. 'The word entrée is a French culinary term signifying a corner or made dish in which sauce is introduced, the importance of which is known in the kitchens of the wealthy as forming the size and magnitude of a dinner; being considered as the principal dish upon which it is intended to dine well, the wealthy epicure orders his cook to prepare a dinner for four, six or eight entrées' (Alexis Soyer, *The Gastronomic Regenerator*, 1846). At dinner at the Royal Pavilion at Brighton on 15 January 1817, guests of the Prince Regent were served with no less than thirty-seven entrées.

With *service à la française* the dishes were placed on the table. A gentleman helped himself and offered to his neighbour the dishes that were within his reach, and requested that other dishes be passed to him either by another diner or a footman. A typical dinner in the early nineteenth century began with a choice of clear or thick soup, both of which were on the table at the same time as the fish. Dishes that replaced others, such as the extra fish dishes that were put on the table in place of the soup, were known as *relevés*, or removes. The entrées, comprising cutlets, fricassées, fricandeaux, fillets, scollops, salmis, boudins, sweetbreads, pâtés-chauds and chartreuses, led on to the roasts. The entremets that followed were cold entrées, dressed vegetables, shellfish and eggs, and also pastries, gâteaux, jellies, creams and other sweets. Dishes that were handed round and never placed on the table were called *assiettes volantes*. Dessert and ices completed the dinner. In Queen Victoria's household it was customary to serve a sorbet, usually flavoured with port, brandy or rum, before the roast to cool and prepare the stomach for the most substantial dishes.

With *service à la russe* (described earlier with regard to the butler and the footman), introduced in the mid-nineteenth century, a smaller number of dishes were served to each diner in turn so that diners were offered each dish in a particular order. Service was from the sideboard, where the joints were carved, and dishes were placed in the centre of the dining-table.

The expertise of the cook was manifested in the delicacies that he or she could prepare but also in the results of careful supervision of the kitchen staff and their work. It was the cook's responsibility to see that the plates were warmed, that each dish was ready on time and that hot food left the kitchen piping hot to be transported by footmen through the passages to the dining-room or to a warming cupboard in the serving room. The kitchen, like the nursery, was situated as far as possible from the main reception rooms, in this case to prevent heat and cooking smells reaching them. It was generally in the basement or a wing of a house, or even in a separate building connected with the dining-room by an underground passage.

Quality did not necessitate extravagance or waste. The kitchen had to be managed, as the advertisement stated, 'with care and economy': goods supplied by tradesmen ordered in the correct quantity and at the best time of year, fresh and in perfect condition when they were delivered or else sent back; the larders kept clean and free from vermin and insects; in the country, before the days of gas and electrical refrigeration, ice brought regularly from the ice house to keep food fresh; the fire or range managed efficiently. Eliza Acton, the author of one of the most influential cookery books of the nineteenth century, wrote that 'It is not, in fact, cookery-books that we need half so much as cooks trained to a knowledge of their duties, and suited, by their acquirements, to families of different grades'.

Instructions and Receipts from the Kitchen, Dairy, Larder and Scullery

GENERAL BUSINESS OF THE LARDER

Joints of meat, game, &c. should be hung where there is a current of dry air, till they are tender. If they be not kept long enough, they will be hard and tough; – if too long, they loose their flavour. Much loss is sustained by the spoiling of meat in warm weather; to prevent which, as far as possible, it must be turned daily, end for end, and wiped every morning and night, with a clean, dry cloth, to free it and keep it from damp and moisture. If it be feared that any of the ripe meat will not keep till wanted, it should be parboiled, or part-roasted, by which means it may be kept a day or two the longer. Pieces of charcoal should also be put over meat, and a plug of charcoal put into the vents of fowls, &c. a string being tied round their necks.

In frosty weather all meats should be brought into the kitchen over night, or at least several hours before it is to be dressed.

Samuel and Sarah Adams, *The Complete Servant*, 1825

TO KEEP FISH HOT FOR TABLE

Never leave it in the water after it is done, but if it cannot be sent to table as soon as it is ready to serve, lift it out, lay the fish-plate into a large and very hot dish, and set it across the fish-kettle; just dip a clean cloth into the boiling water, and spread it upon the fish, place a tin cover over it, and let it remain so until or three minutes before it is wanted, then remove the cloth, and put the fish back into the kettle for an instant that it may be as hot as possible: drain, dish, and serve it immediately: the water should be kept boiling the whole time.

Eliza Acton, *Modern Cookery for Private Families*, 1856

TO CHOOSE FISH

The cook should be well acquainted with the signs of freshness and good condition in fish, as they are most unwholesome articles of food when stale, and many of them are also dangerous eating when they are out of season. The eyes should always be bright, the gills of a fine clear red, the body stiff, the flesh firm, yet elastic to the touch, and the smell not disagreeable. When all these marks are reversed, and the eyes are sunken, the gills very dark in hue, the fish itself flabby and of offensive odour, it is bad, and should be avoided.

Lobsters, prawns, and shrimps, are very stiff when freshly boiled, and the tails turn strongly inwards; when these relax, and the fish are soft and watery, they are stale; and the smell will detect their being so, instantly, even if no other symptoms of it be remarked. If bought alive, lobsters should be chosen by their weight and 'liveliness'. The hen lobster is preferred for sauce and soups, on account of the coral; but the flesh of the male is generally considered of finer flavour for eating. The vivacity of their leaps will show when prawns and shrimps are fresh from the sea.

Eliza Acton, *Modern Cookery for Private Families*, 1856

TO CLARIFY STOCK

INGREDIENTS.– *The whites of 2 eggs, ¹/₂ pint of water, 2 quarts of stock.*

Mode.– Supposing that by some accident the soup is not quite clear, and that its quantity is 2 quarts, take the whites of 2 eggs, carefully separated from their yolks, whisk them well together with the water, and add gradually the 2 quarts of boiling stock, still whisking. Place the soup on the fire, and when boiling and well skimmed, whisk the eggs with it till nearly boiling again; then draw it from the fire, and let it settle, until the whites of the eggs become separated. Pass through a fine cloth, and the soup should be clear.

Note.– The rule is, that all clear soups should be of a light straw-colour, and should not savour too strongly of the meat; and that all white or brown thick soups should have no more consistency than will enable them to adhere slightly to the spoon when hot. All *purees* should be somewhat thicker.

Mrs Isabella Beeton, *The Book of Household Management*, 1861

OYSTERS

(In season from September to April)

The old-fashioned plan of *feeding* oysters with a sprinkling of oatmeal or flour, in addition to the salt and water to which they were committed, has long been rejected by all genuine amateurs of these nutritious and excellent fish, who consider the plumpness which the oysters are supposed to gain from the process, but poor compensation for the flavour from the beds, and to keep them in good condition for four or five days, they only require to be covered with cold water, with five ounces of salt to the gallon dissolved in it before it is poured on them; this should be changed with regularity every twenty-four hours. By following this plan with exactness they may be kept alive from a week to ten days, but will remain in perfect condition scarcely more than half that time. Oysters should be eaten always the instant they are opened. Abroad they are served before the soup in the first course of a dinner, arranged usually in as many plates as there are guests at table. In England they are sometimes served *after* the soup. A sense of *appropriateness* must determine how far the variations of fashion should be followed in such matters.

Eliza Acton, *Modern Cookery for Private Families*, 1856

YORKSHIRE CREAM CHEESE

Take any quantity of cream and put it into a wet cloth. Tie it up, and hang it in a cool place for seven or eight days. Then take it from the cloth and put it into a mould (in another cloth) with a weight upon it, for two or three days longer. Turn it twice a day, when it will be fit for use.

Mrs Loudon, *The Lady's Country Companion*, 1845

BATH CREAM CHEESE

Add half a pint of cream to a quart of new milk, and warm the mixture till it is about 80° of Fahrenheit; then stir in as much rennet as will coagulate it. As soon as the curd has formed, put a cloth over the bottom of a large shallow vat, and, taking the curd up with a skimming-dish, place it in the vat and wrap the cloth over it. As the curd shrinks, the vat must be filled up with fresh curd, till the cheese is of a proper thickness. When the cheese has become a little firm, it is turned out of the vat and laid in a dry cloth. A board is then put over it, on which is placed a weight of two pounds. At night it is put into another clean cloth, and the next morning it is slightly salted with a little fine dry salt, and placed on a bed of fresh nettles or strawberry leaves, being covered with leaves of the same kind. These leaves are changed every morning, and the cheese is turned twice a day for a fortnight, after which it is fit for use.

Mrs Loudon, *The Lady's Country Companion*, 1845

TO KEEP CELERY FRESH

Keep celery fresh by rolling it in brown paper sprinkled with water, then in a damp cloth, and putting it then in a cool, dark place. Before preparing it for the table, submerge it in cold water, and let it stand for an hour. It will then be found very crisp.

Things a Woman Wants to Know

TO MAKE BUTTER

During summer, skim the milk when the sun has not heated the dairy; at that season it should stand for butter twenty-four hours without skimming, and forty-eight in winter. Deposit the cream pot in a very cool cellar if your dairy is not more so. If you cannot churn daily, change it into scalding fresh pots; but never omit churning twice a week. If possible, put the churn in a thorough air; and if not a barrel one, set it in a tub of water two feet deep, which will give firmness to the butter.– When the butter is come, pour off the butter-milk, and put the butter into a fresh scalded pan, or tubs which have afterwards been in cold water. Pour water on it, and let it lie to acquire some hardness before you work it; then change the water, and beat it with flat boards so perfectly, that not the least taste of the butter-milk remains, and that the water, used should be quite clear in colour. Then work some salt into it, weigh and make it into forms, throw them into cold water in an earthen pan and cover of the queen's ware. You will then have very nice cool butter in the hottest weather: but neither should be left with a particle of buttermilk or a sour taste, as is sometimes done.

M. E. Reynolds, *The Complete Art of Cookery*, 1848

TO PRESERVE BUTTER

Make a good brine. Boil two pounds of salt, six lumps of sugar, and as much saltpetre as will lie on a shilling in one gallon of water for ten minutes. When cold, wrap each pat of butter in wet muslin or cloth, and put it into the brine. The butter must always remain under the surface of the brine, and then it will keep good for months, and a pat can be taken out as required.

Domestic Life, 1897

TO MAKE YEAST

It may be made by putting a teacupful of split peas into a basin and pouring about a pint of boiling water over them. A cloth is then put over the basin, and it is set near the fire to keep warm. In about twelve hours it will begin to ferment, and a kind of scum will rise, which may be used as yeast. This is called Turkish yeast; but a better method is practised by the Americans, which is as follows:– Take as much hops as may be held between the thumb and finger, put them with a few slices of apples into a quart of water, and boil the whole for about fifteen minutes or twenty minutes. Then strain the liquid, and when it is lukewarm stir in a little flour with three or four table-spoonfuls of treacle so as to make a thin paste; then set the whole in a warm place, and in a few hours the fermentation will be sufficiently strong to allow enough flour and water to be added to make a proper sponge for bread.

If you have a small quantity of yeast it may be increased in the following manner:– Take one pound of fine flour, and mix it to the thickness of gruel with boiling water; add half a pound of brown sugar, mixing the whole well together. Then put three tablespoonfuls of yeast into a large vessel, and pour the mixture upon it. It will ferment violently, and the scum which rises to the top will be good yeast, which may be used immediately, or may be preserved for some time in an earthenware vessel covered closely from the air, and kept in a warm dry place.

To keep home-brewed yeast it should be put into a large pan and have three times the quantity of water poured upon it, being well stirred up and then left to settle. The next day the water is to be poured off, and fresh put on, and in this manner it is said that yeast may be kept for six weeks. All yeast is best purified before it is used; that is, the yeast should be put into a vessel, and, cold spring water being poured upon it, they should be stirred together and then left to settle. The water is afterwards poured off, and the yeast taken out carefully, leaving a brown sediment at the bottom.

Mrs Loudon, *The Lady's Country Companion*, 1845

TO KEEP BREAD

Bread requires almost as much care as milk to preserve it wholesome and fresh. It should be laid, as soon as it is perfectly cold, into a large earthen pan with a cover, which should be kept free from crumbs, and be frequently scalded, and then wiped very dry for use. Loaves which have been cut should have a smaller pan appropriated to them, and this also should have the loose crumbs wiped from it daily. It is a good plan to raise the bread-pans from the floor of the larder, when there is no proper stand or frame for the purpose, by means of two flat wedges of wood, so as to allow a current of air to pass under them.

Eliza Acton, *Modern Cookery for Private Families*, 1856

TO FRESHEN STALE BREAD (AND PASTRY, ETC.), AND PRESERVE IT FROM MOULD

If entire loaves be placed in a gentle oven and heated quite through, *without* being previously dipped into cold water, according to the old-fashioned plan, they will eat almost like bread newly baked: they should not remain in it long enough to become hard and dry, but they should be made hot throughout. In very damp localities, when large household bakings take place but once in eight or ten days, it is sometimes necessary to use precautions against the attack of mould, though the bread may have been exceedingly well made; and the method recommended above will be the best for warding it off, and for preserving the bread eatable for several days longer than it would otherwise be. If *large* loaves be just dipped into cold water and then placed in a quick oven until they are again thoroughly dried, they will resemble *new* bread altogether.

Pastry, cakes and biscuits, may all be greatly improved when stale, by heating them in a gentle oven.

Eliza Acton, *Modern Cookery for Private Families*, 1856

TO CURE HAM

For a ham twenty-four pounds in weight, take two ounces of saltpetre, half a pound of common salt, one pound of bay salt, and one ounce of black pepper. Mix these together, and rub them well into the ham; then let it stand three days, and at the expiration of that time pour one pound of treacle over it, and let it remain twenty-four hours; after that time, let it be turned every day for a month, and each time rub the liquor well into it. After this, steep the ham in cold water for twelve hours, then dry it well and hang it up. It will not require any further steeping when it is to be boiled; and it should be boiled slowly, say at the rate of about three hours for a ham of the weight of ten pounds.

Mrs Loudon, *The Lady's Country Companion*, 1845

PARSLEY

Instead of keeping parsley in water, which makes it turn yellow, put it in an air-tight jar in a cool place. This will keep it fresh for some time.

Things a Woman Wants to Know

THE SMELL OF ONIONS

Mustard-water will cleanse the hands from all odour after peeling onions.

Things a Woman Wants to Know

THE MANNER OF CURING WILTSHIRE BACON

Sprinkle each flitch with salt, and let the blood drain off for twenty-four hours; then mix a pound and a half of coarse sugar, the same quantity of bay-salt, not quite so much as half a pound of saltpetre, and a pound of common salt; and rub this well on the bacon, turning it every day for a month: then hang it to dry, and afterwards smoke it ten days. This quantity of salts is sufficient for the whole hog.

A New System of Domestic Cookery, 1860

VEGETABLES

Vegetables should be carefully cleaned from insects and well washed in a large quantity of water in an earthen pan, as sand and dust are apt to hang round wooden vessels. The water should boil before they are put in, and a little salt added, or a tea-spoonful of salt of wormwood, to preserve their colour. Boil them quickly in a tinned saucepan by themselves in plenty of water, but do not cover them: if the water has not slackened in boiling, they are done when they begin to sink. Take them out immediately, or the colour will change. Carrots and turnips may be boiled with meat, without injury to either: but carrots must not be boiled with any thing you wish to look white. All kinds of vegetables should have a little crispness, and therefore must not be boiled too much.

The Housekeeper's Receipt Book,
1813

EELS

Kill them by knocking their heads upon a block or anything hard; then take the head in your hand with a cloth, and just cut through the skin round the neck, and turn it down about an inch; then pull the head with one hand and the skin with the other, it will come off with facility; open the belly and take out the inside; cut off the fins and those bristles that run up the back; if the eel is large and oily, hold it over a charcoal fire, moving it quickly all the while; but the small ones will not require it. Nothing is harder to kill than eels; and it is only by killing, or rather stunning them in the manner above described that they suffer the least.

Alexis Soyer, *The Gastronomic Regenerator,* 1846

TO SMOKE HERRINGS

Clean, and lay them in salt and a little saltpetre one night; then hang them on a stick, through the eyes, in a row. Have ready an old cask, on which put some sawdust, and in the midst of it a heater red hot: fix the stick over the smoke, and let them remain 24 hours.

A New System of Domestic Cookery, 1860

IRON POTS

To cure cracks or fissures in iron pots or pans, mix some finely sifted lime with white of eggs well beaten, till reduced to a paste, then add some iron file dust, and apply the composition to the injured part; it will soon become hard and fit for use.

The Housekeeper's Receipt Book, 1813

TO CLEAN THE BACK OF THE GRATE, THE INNER HEARTH, AND THE FRONTS OF CAST-IRON STOVES

Boil about a quarter of a pound of the best black lead with a pint of small beer, and a bit of soap the size of a walnut. When that is melted, dip a painter's brush, and wet the grate, having first brushed off all the soot and dust; then take a hard brush, and rub it till of a beautiful brightness.

A New System of Domestic Cookery,
1860

COALS

Judicious Cooks will perform their culinary operations with much less coal than those who erroneously conceive that the greater the fire, the greater the dispatch. *Time,* rather than a fierce fire, answers *best* both for roasting and boiling meats. – Round coals are best for use, and small coal should never be thrown on a weak fire, as it will stop the progress of the air through the fire; and perhaps extinguish it. But small coal, or culm, a little wetted, and thrown at the back of a good fire, will become cinders or coke, and greatly improve it.

All the ashes of the kitchen and other grates should be sifted, and the cinders saved, to be used under the boilers in brewing and washing, or in the ironing stove.

Samuel and Sarah Adams, *The Complete Servant,* 1825

TO CLEAN WOODEN TABLES

Mix together two ounces of soda, a quarter of a pound of soft soap, and half a pound of fuller's earth, with enough boiling water to make it into a paste.

Things a Woman Wants to Know

TO TAKE THE BLACK OFF THE BRIGHT BARS OF POLISHED STOVES IN A FEW MINUTES

Rub them well with some of the following mixture on a bit of broad cloth; when the dirt is removed, wipe them clean, and polish with glass, not sand-paper.

The mixture – Boil slowly one pound of soft soap in two quarts of water, to one. Of this jelly take three or four spoonfuls, and mix to a consistence with emery, No 3.

A New System of Domestic Cookery, 1860

PEWTER AND TIN

Dish-covers and pewter requisites should be wiped dry immediately after being used, and kept free from steam or damp, which would prevent much of the trouble in cleaning them. Where the polish is gone off, let the articles be first rubbed on the outside with a little sweet oil laid on a piece of soft linen cloth: then clear it off with pure whitening on linen cloths, which will restore the polish.

The Housekeeper's Receipt Book, 1813

TO BROWN THE SURFACE OF A DISH WITHOUT BAKING OR PLACING IT AT THE FIRE

This is done with a salamander, as it is called; it is heated in the fire, and held over the dish sufficiently near to give it colour. It is very much used in a superior order of cookery. A kitchen shovel is sometimes substituted for it in an emergency.

Eliza Acton, *Modern Cookery for Private Families*, 1856

PICKLE FOR THE BRINE TROUGH

The pickle for the large brine trough is made by mixing four gallons of water with a pound or a pound and a half of coarse sugar, four ounces of saltpetre, and six pounds of common or bay salt. This mixture should be boiled in a large kettle, and the scum taken off as it rises. When no more scum appears, the vessel should be taken from the fire, and the liquid suffered to stand still till it is cold.

It is said that meat may be kept in this pickle for twelve months, provided the pickle be boiled and skimmed about once in two months, and that during the boiling two ounces of sugar and half a pound of salt be added. In general, the articles which have been salted, after remaining about a fortnight or three weeks in the pickle, are taken out and hung up to dry. Some persons lay them to drain, and then hang them up without any other preparation; but others advise them to be wiped quite dry and put in paper bags before they are hung up. Whenever fresh articles are put into the pickle, every thing should be taken out of the trough, and the brine boiled up, the scum being taken off and fresh salt and sugar added, as before directed. Sometimes meat is merely salted when it is to be used in a few days; in which case the meat is put into a smaller trough or pan, and only salt is used in the proportion of a quarter of a pound of salt to every two pounds of meat. The salt should be well rubbed in, and the meat turned every day.

Mrs Loudon, *The Lady's Country Companion*, 1845

TO PLUCK AND DRAW POULTRY

To pluck either game or poultry have the bird upon a board with its head towards you, and pull the feathers away from you, which is the direction they lay in; many persons pull out the feathers in a contrary direction, by which means they are likely to tear the skin to pieces, which would very much disfigure the bird for the table.

To draw poultry after it is well plucked, cut a long incision at the back of the neck, cut the neck bone off close to the body of the bird, but leave the skin a good length over, then take out the thin skin from under the outer with the crop, cut an incision under the tail just large enough for the gizzard to pass through, no larger, then put your finger into the bird at the breast and detach all the intestines, squeeze the body of the bird and force out the whole from the incision at the tail.

Alexis Soyer, *The Gastronomic Regenerator*, 1846

CURLED BUTTER

Tie a strong cloth by two of the corners to an iron hook in the wall; make a knot with the other two ends, so that a stick might pass through. Put the butter into the cloth; twist it tightly over a dish into which the butter will fall through the knot, so forming small and pretty little strings. The butter may then be garnished with parsley, if to serve with a cheese course; or it may be sent to table plain for breakfast, in an ornamental dish. Squirted butter for garnishing hams, salads, eggs, &c., is made by forming a piece of stiff paper in the shape of a cornet, and squeezing the butter in fine strings from the hole at the bottom. Scooped butter is made by dipping a teaspoon or scooper in warm water, and then scooping the butter quickly and thin. In warm weather, it would not be necessary to heat the spoon.

Mrs Isabella Beeton, *The Book of Household Management*, 1861

TO PRESERVE EGGS

Apply with a brush a solution of gum-arabic to the shells, or immerse the eggs therein, let them dry, and afterwards pack them in dry charcoal dust. This prevents their being affected by any alterations of temperature.

James W. Laughton, *The General Receipt-Book*, c. 1845

CURDS AND WHEY

Rennet is generally prepared for dairy-use by butchers, and kept in farm-houses hung in the chimney corners, where it will remain good a long time. It is the inner stomach of the calf, from which the curd is removed, and which is salted and stretched out to dry on splinters of wood, or strong wooden skewers. It should be preserved from dust and smoke (by a paper-bag or other means), and portions of it cut off as wanted. Soak a small bit in half a teacupful of warm water, and let it remain in it for an hour or two; then pour into a quart of warm new milk a dessertspoonful of rennet-liquor, and keep it in a warm place until the whey appears separated from the curd, and looks clear. The smaller the proportion of rennet used, the more soft and delicate will be the curd. We write these directions from recollection, having often had the dish thus prepared, but having no memorandum at this moment of the precise proportions used. Less than an inch square of the rennet would be sufficient, we think, for a gallon of milk, if some hours were allowed for it to turn. When *rennet-whey*, which is a most valuable beverage in many cases of illness, is required for an invalid to drink, a bit of the rennet, after being quickly and slightly rinsed, may be stirred at once into the warm milk, as the curd becoming hard is then of no consequence. It must be kept warm until the whey appears and is clear. It may then be strained, and given to the patient to drink, or allowed to become cold before it is taken. In feverish complaints it has often the most benign effect.

Eliza Acton, *Modern Cookery for Private Families*, 1856

TO SWEETEN MEAT, FISH &C. THAT IS TAINTED

When meat, fish, &c. from intense heat, or long keeping, are likely to pass into a state of corruption, a simple and pure mode of keeping them sound and healthful is by putting a few pieces of charcoal, each the size of an egg, into the pot or saucepan wherein the meat or fish is to be boiled. Among others, an experiment of this kind was tried upon a turbot, which appeared too far gone to be eatable; the cook, as advised, put four pieces of charcoal under the strainer in the fish kettle; after boiling the proper time, the turbot came to the table perfectly sweet and clean.

The Modern Family Receipt Book, 1831

TO DISCOVER WHETHER FLOUR BE ADULTERATED WITH WHITENING OR CHALK

Mix with the flour some juice of lemon or good vinegar; if the flour is pure, they will remain together at rest, but if there be a mixture of whitening or chalk, a fermentation or working like yeast will ensue. The adulterated meal is whiter and heavier than the good. The quantity that an ordinary tea-cup will contain, has been found to weigh more than the quantity of genuine flour by four drachms and nineteen grains troy.

The School or Arts; or, Fountain of Knowledge

BOILING VEGETABLES

The boiling of green vegetables may be expedited, the colour preserved, and if they are old and tough, they may be tender, by putting in with them a *small quantity* of soda: half a teaspoonful of carbonate of soda, or a bit of washing soda, the size of a small hazelnut, is enough for a moderate dressing. This is not suitable for potatoes or roots in general, it spoils their colour, though it improves that of greens.

Esther Copley, *Cottage Cookery*, 1849

DISHING UP

Let a clean cloth be laid on the kitchen-table, and with the *bill of fare* for your guide, if neither housekeeper nor the butler be present, let the dishes, intended to be used, be placed on this table, exactly as they are meant to stand on the table in the dining-room, and let every article be taken off the table in the kitchen, by the footman, and proper assistants, in regular order, by which means the butler cannot fail to set them in their proper places above stairs.

Samuel and Sarah Adams, *The Complete Servant*, 1825

FORCEMEAT OF VEAL

Take a pound and a half of lean veal, scrape, pound, and pass it through a fine wire sieve, when passed there should be one pound of meat; then take one pound of beef suet, which shred and chop very fine, put it into a mortar and pound it well, then add six ounces of panade, with the suet, pound them well together; then add the veal, season with a little pepper, salt, and a very little grated nutmeg, mix the whole well together; then add three eggs by degrees, then the yolks of three more eggs when well mixed, whisk the whites of the three eggs to a very stiff froth, add to the forcemeat, mix them well in, and it is ready to use where directed. To form this....into large quenelles, have two silver tablespoons, fill one of them with the forcemeat, dip your knife in hot water with which smooth it over, then dip the other spoon into boiling water, and with it remove the forcemeat from the first spoon and slip it from that into a buttered sauté pan, proceeding thus until you have as many as you require; then cover them with some second stock, and boil them about ten minutes, or until firm, and they are ready for use. Small quenelles are made in the same manner, only using teaspoons instead of tablespoons.

Alexis Soyer, *The Gastronomic Regenerator*, 1846

The Children's Nurse and Nursery Maid

This important servant ought to be of a lively and cheerful disposition, perfectly good tempered, and clean and neat in her habits and person', wrote Samuel and Sarah Adams of the children's nurse. This was echoed by Mrs Beeton, who claimed patience, equability, minute cleanliness and purity of manners to be her essential qualities. 'Every bad quality in the nurse is reproduced in children with painful accuracy. The nursery is oftener than not the children's world; their mother is to them the beautiful lady whom they see ten minutes during the day, and whose visits to the nursery are of the briefest; when this is so, the influence of the nurse is supreme over the minds of her charges', wrote the author of *The Servants' Practical Guide*.

A well-born child of the seventeenth century was generally cared for by his mother with the help of a gentlewoman who was either a friend, an unmarried member of the family or one who had fallen on hard times. Later, as the mistress began to delegate more and more the running of her house to a house steward or housekeeper, it became the custom to hand over completely the upbringing of her children to a responsible servant. The children's nurse of the eighteenth and nineteenth centuries was often the daughter of a trusted retainer and not of gentle birth. Traditionally she was the eldest of a large family, accustomed to looking after her younger brothers and sisters and helping her mother, and she began in service as a nursery maid at the age of twelve or thirteen. She left home to make room for the younger members of her own family as they grew up and to reduce the number of mouths for her parents to feed.

The head nurse, sometimes known as 'Nursey' or 'Nanny', was

assisted by an under nurse and nursery maids proportionate to the number of her charges and according to the family's means. Entrusted with the early upbringing of the 'hopes of the family' – boys who would continue the line and girls who might one day make good marriages – her responsibilities were considerable. Whereas the other household servants were principally employed in making agreeable the existence of their master and mistress, the task of the nurse was to relieve them of some of their obligations.

In a well-to-do Victorian family a child would be placed in the charge of a nurse as soon as he was weaned from his mother or wet-nurse. He remained in the nursery until the age of five, or sometimes longer, when he would begin to spend his mornings in the school room under the supervision of a tutor or governess. At this moment boys ceased to be dressed like girls in pretty frocks and coloured sashes and were 'breeched'.

The author of *The Servants' Practical Guide*, dismayed by the accents and vulgar speech of children left in the charge of an uneducated person,

recommended to parents of the 1880s the seventeenth-century practice of employing a 'young-lady nurse', more often known as a nursery-governess in the Victorian period: 'The diction of a nurse is also of serious importance to the children under her care; if she is an uneducated woman, she mispronounces and miscalls almost every word she utters, and the children, with all the quickness of childhood, contact habits of speech which are subsequently difficult to overcome. Others, again, display a great disregard for the letter H, or perhaps a misplaced affection for it; and although it may amuse the members of the family when she talks of Master 'Enery's beautiful blue heyes, it is not perhaps quite so amusing when Master Henry himself informs his mamma's visitors that he has "'urt his 'ead" and "Pinched his 'and".'

Other writers, and presumably parents, were equally concerned with the health of children.

Speak gently to the little child,
Its love be sure to gain;
Teach it in accents soft and
  mild;
It may not long remain!

Speak gently to the young, for they
Will have enough to bear;
Pass through this world as best
  they may
'Tis full of anxious care.

The lines, taken from *A Few Hints to Nursemaids*, allude lightheartedly to the pains of childhood in the nineteenth century and to the frequent occurrence of death in the nursery. In 1868, for instance, it was estimated that twenty-six out of every hundred children died before they reached the age of five.

Costiveness was generally thought to be a symptom, if not the cause, of a multitude of childish complaints and the most potent laxatives were prescribed for quite young children. Mrs Beeton's purgative consisted of scammony and jalap (both vegetables substances) and powdered antimony, to which Syrup of Violets recommended by the Adams must certainly have been preferable. Another, described in the magazine *The Housekeeper*, was known to be so violent in its effect that vomiting was a common consequence. Remedies for thrush, hooping-cough (or chincough)and other ailments of infancy frequently contained poisonous substances and may have accounted for a number of nursery tragedies. Mrs Beeton's tonic for a child recuperating from measles, for example, was composed of an infusion of rose leaves, quinine and sulphuric acid.

Convulsions indicated the onset of illness and were also to be expected when a child was teething, according to several nineteenth-century authorities on the rearing of children. When the pain of dentition was acute, some advisers thought it preferable to apply leeches to lance the gums than to administer sleep-inducing laudanum. Despite doctors' warnings, lethal quantities of narcotics and alcohol were given to infants by callous nurses hoping for a peaceful night's sleep, or when they wanted to slip downstairs for a gossip in the housekeeper's room or the servants' hall.

The relationship of the nursery staff with the other household servants was often uneasy. Demands rather than polite negotiations were made for special food for the children – eggs at unusual times and milk sent back to be reboiled – encouraging conflict with the kitchen staff. The nurseries were usually situated on an upper floor or in a wing of a country house, as far as possible from the grown-ups and separated from them by a wooden gate on the landing or better still a long passage and a stout door. Footmen on nursery duty generally disliked the fetching and carrying of meals and messages, especially the communications sent to or from the kitchen.

Lunch in the Victorian nursery traditionally consisted of boiled mutton and milk pudding. Watched over by the nurse and nursery maids, the younger children were taught not to put their elbows on the table and to eat every morsel on their plates (unless it was a nursery where it was a rule to leave a little for Mr Manners). A typical punishment for failing to eat up was to present the young offender with the reject food at each subsequent meal until it was consumed.

A properly brought-up young lady would have learned at a very early age that soup must be eaten from the side, not the point, of the spoon and the noise caused by inhaling air when supping was ill-mannered. A young gentleman would have no need to be reminded not to tip his glass as if he were going to stand it upside down on his nose. He was taught in the nursery that the glass should be brought perpendicularly to the lips and then lifted at a slight angle.

As an upper servant, the head nurse enjoyed the privilege of a place at the housekeeper's table in the evening, but she might prefer to have her supper sent up to the nursery. Whether or not she was on friendly terms with the housekeeper, she was apt to maintain an air of detached self-importance in her company, either, in the case of a nursery-governess, because she was of superior background and education or because she felt that she enjoyed a closer relationship to her mistress through being entrusted with the care of the children.

However rare the appearance of the children's parents in the nursery, the descent of the children to the dining-room or drawing-room was a custom accepted by even the most uninterested parents. At the period when dinner was early in the evening, the children joined the grown-ups for dessert and were fed sweetmeats from the table as a reward for good manners or well-learned lessons. By the mid-nineteenth century, when dinner was at the later time of seven or eight in the evening, the visit took place in the drawing-room after tea. Scrubbed and brushed and wearing crisply ironed clothes, the children were despatched downstairs, some eager, some nervous at leaving the security of the nursery. All but the vainest were irked by the preparations, which involved the nursery maids in endless fumbling with tiny mother-of-pearl buttons. The older children were taken to the door by a nursery maid, while the head nurse brought down the baby of the family, equally elaborately got up for the brief appearance.

Upstairs again, the nursery maids prepared the children's baths. Before the days of running water a hip bath in front to the nursery fire was filled with hot water brought up in brass cans. Once the children were settled there were boots and slippers to be polished and sewing, mending and altering to be done. The children's underclothes and night clothes were generally made in the nursery, and sometimes their everyday clothes, too.

In the morning the most junior nursery maid rose at six to sweep and dust the day nursery, clean the grate and light the fire. She laid the table for breakfast with the special nursery china and took tea to the head nurse. The baby was exclusively in the charge of the head nurse and usually slept in a cradle in her room. The older children were attended to by the under nurse and nursery maids, who dressed them, took them down to family prayers after breakfast and afterwards for a walk if they were too young for the schoolroom. They put them to rest before lunch and after lunch took them out again, often accompanying the head nurse carrying the baby in her arms or pushing him in a perambulator.

Perambulators did not make their appearance until the middle of the nineteenth century. They looked at first like miniature bath chairs in which the child sat rather than lay. By 1887 a 'bassinette-perambulator', in which an infant of less than six months could lie comfortably at full length instead of being strapped into a sitting posture, was being recommended. Nurses were severely warned that bumping a child's carriage over kerbs and up and down the porch or area steps of a town house could cause brain and spine damage. The child was not to be treated 'like a calf in a cart going to slaughter', to quote from *Counsel to a Mother on the Care and Rearing of her Children*, and some nurses at the end of the Victorian period still preferred to walk with the baby in their arms. The vehicle itself was a status symbol. The most expensive and up-to-date models contributed to the prestige of the nurse and were as much a sign that she had a good position as the smartness of the clothes worn by her charges.

Although money might be spent on the perambulator and the children's clothes, the day and night nurseries were rarely furnished with anything better than pieces rejected from elsewhere in the house. Summer and winter there was usually a fire burning in the grate in the day nursery, protected by a tall brass-railed fire-guard on which clothes were hung to be aired. There would be a table and chairs — a high chair for the baby — for meals, and perhaps a rocking chair for the nurse. The draught from the door might be shut out by a folding screen decorated with pictures of animals and flowers and royalty, in particular royal children, cut out of magazines. Reproductions of paintings, usually of a religious, heroic or whimsical character, might hang on the walls.

No nursery was complete without a rocking horse and a doll's house, often made by the estate carpenter and passed on from one generation of children to the next. Also the work of a craftsman was the Noah's ark with its carved wooden animals in pairs. This was the only toy permitted on Sundays in some Victorian nurseries.

By the early nineteenth century a number of commercially made games and toys were to be bought, including a great variety of dolls. These were thought to encourage a girl to be gentle and useful as well as giving her 'pleasure unthinkable'. In her childhood at Kensington Palace Queen Victoria had one hundred and thirty-two dolls.

The nursery maids, the younger ones scarcely more than children themselves, took part in nursery games in and out of doors. They taught the children to skip and bowl a hoop, helped with dressing-up and acting games and, when they were fretful or quarrelsome, read (if they could) or told the children stories. The head nurse would have tales to tell of her own childhood.

There was nothing to compare with the devotion of a kindly nurse to the children she had brought up and cared for. Her loyalty was with them through all the ups and downs of their grown-up lives and extended unquestioningly to their children. In retirement, she alone of the household servants might remain on in the house, still occupying her nurseries and keeping them in readiness for the time when the next generation of children would visit their grandparents. The affection she inspired is illustrated in the words of a child of nine:

Children are the chief delight
Of Nanny, my Nanny.
She always sleeps with them at
    night
And seldom lets them out of
    sight,
Does Nanny, my Nanny.

Nanny mends the baby's frock,
Does Nanny, my Nanny.
And tightens the neck of her
    new smock,
And always winds up the nursery
    clock,
Does Nanny, my Nanny.

She feeds the rabbits when I'm
    in bed,
Does Nanny, my Nanny.
I'm sure they're kept fat and
    well fed
And always have lots of straw for
    their bed
With Nanny, my Nanny.

Nanny knits gloves for the oth-
    ers and me,
Does Nanny, my Nanny.
How she does it I never can see;
But a sweeter old Nanny could
    never be
Than our dear Nanny.

Instructions and Receipts from the Nursery

THE CRADLE

The cradle should be *large*, and the head lined, but without the addition of curtains; the first mattress should be of hair, the upper one of fine wool; the pillow of downy feathers well filled; the covering should consist of a fine blanket, bound round with a broad binding of very fine calico muslin; the coverlid of fine calico. On placing the child in the cradle, the pillow should be levelled, and a thick soft blanket doubled several times to prevent the mattress being wetted. As the infant advances, a very soft morocco leather to cover the mattress under the flannel is necessary; as every possible care should be observed to keep the cradle delicately nice. The nurse should be careful in covering the child, to simply lay the clothes lightly over it, leaving the child at full liberty to move about.– The cradle may well be objected to when improperly managed.

The Good Nurse, 1828

CORDIAL GRIPE-WATER FOR BABIES

Take Aniseed water, one ounce
   Pure water, one pint
   Treacle, two table spoonfuls
   Tincture of opium, three drachms

A tea spoonful or two may be given occasionally. It is equal in goodness to the best Godfrey's Cordial.

The Modern Family Receipt Book, 1831

OINTMENT TO HEAL SORES ON CHILDREN'S CHINS AND EARS

Take White lead, four drachms
   Red Lead, two drachms
Linseed oil and spirits of turpentine sufficient to form a liniment. Lay it on with a feather, twice a day, and the sores will disappear in a week.

The Modern Family Receipt Book, 1831

FORCING THE MIND

A healthy child's mind should lie fallow, so far as alphabet and books are concerned, until five years old. Delicate and nervous children may thus be neglected until the age of six or seven years, without danger of duncehood.

Marion Harland, *Common Sense in the Nursery*, 1887

BREAD JELLY

Take off the crust of five slices of stale bread, then toast them a light brown. Put them into two quarts of boiling water, with a few slices of lemon; let it boil to a jelly; then strain and sweeten to the taste. To be eaten cold. If the lemon is not liked, the jelly can be flavoured with a little wine, put in at the same time with the sugar. A very delicate article of diet.

N. E. Davies, *Nursery Hints*, 1884

GREEN IN THE NURSERY

Avoid green in choosing ribbons for Baby's sashes, caps, and dress-trimmings. The prettiest shades of this colour are made up with ingredients which are distinctly arsenical. Watch him as closely as you may, the child is apt to get the end of the sash or cap-string in his mouth, in which case the stain on lips, tongue, and frock is the least harmful consequence. Babies have been thrown into paroxysms of vomiting by chewing green ribbon, and more than one case of skin-poisoning has been caused by wearing hats or hoods tied under the chin with strings of the same, the perspiration facilitating absorption of the poisonous dye. In the knowledge of these facts physicians object to green wall-papers in nurseries and in sleeping-rooms.

Marion Harland, *Common Sense in the Nursery*, 1887

CLOTHES

Now in getting warmth without weight we should use woollen garments, remembering that wool is a poor conductor of heat, and so necessarily retains the heat longer than any other material. Heat is conducted slower in loosely woven materials than in close; therefore wool loosely woven is warmer than that which is closely woven. Loose-fitting garments are warmer than tight ones. Linen is the best conductor of heat. Woollen garments give the best protection against sudden changes of temperatures. It is usual to have outer garments made of linen, but woollen garments should be beneath.

J. J. Marsh, *Nursery Handbook*, 1891

CHILDREN'S CLOTHES

The colour of a child's clothes is an important consideration; the colour in winter ought to be dark, as dark coloured clothes are much warmer than light; while he should, on the other hand, wear in the summer season light-coloured clothes; and, if the weather be extremely hot, perfectly white dresses.

P. H. Chavasse, *Counsel to a Mother on the Care and Rearing of her Children*, 1874

CONVULSIONS

If medical attendance cannot be procured, the child should be put in a hot bath (temperature 100°F) and a good purgative given to clear out the bowels and relieve the head.

N. E. Davies, *Nursery Hints*, 1884

HICCUPS

These generally arise from acidity in the stomach, and may be remedied by the administration of eight grains of prepared chalk, with two grains of powdered rhubarb, given in a little syrup, or gruel. If very severe, the stomach is to be rubbed with soap liniment, or opodeldoc, to which a little laudanum has been added.

Samuel and Sarah Adams, *The Complete Servant*, 1825

COPYING OF MUSLIN PATTERNS

The drawing is to be placed on a sheet of white paper, and the outline pricked through with a pin: the white sheet may then be laid on a second clear one, and a muslin bag of mixed charcoal sifted or rubbed over it. The pierced paper being removed, a perfect copy will be traced on the other; and in this way patterns may be multiplied very expeditiously.

The Housekeeper's Receipt Book, 1813

CHILBLAIN LOTION

Take one drachm of sugar of lead, and two of white vitriol, reduce them to a fine powder, and add four ounces of water. Before using this lotion, it is to be well shaken, then rubbed well on the parts affected, before a good fire, with the hand. The best time for application is in the evening. It scarcely ever fails curing the most inveterate chilblains by once or twice using. It is not to be used on broken chilblains.

The Modern Family Receipt Book, 1831

FOR A BRUISED EYE

Take conserve of red roses and rotten apple in equal quantities, wrap them in a fold of thin cambric, or old linen, and apply it to the eye; it will relieve the bruise and remove the blackness.

Samuel and Sarah Adams, *The Complete Servant*, 1825

DUSTING POWDER

Those parts coming constantly in close contact require to be frequently sponged with tepid water, and afterwards made dry with a soft cloth; when perfectly dry, they should be dusted with equal parts of Fuller's-earth and prepared chalk, tied up in a piece of clear muslin.

The Good Nurse, 1828

DOLLS

Let a girl have dolls in abundance, all sorts and sizes, expensive and inexpensive. They make her gentle and useful, and give her pleasure unspeakable. They make her gentle; and what is more beautiful in the fair sex than gentleness? They make her useful: the dressing and undressing of her dolls make her handy and lissom; the cutting-out, the fitting, and the sewing of her dolls' dresses, make her clever with the needle; the nursing of her dolls early initiates her into the mysteries of handling, of fondling, and soothing a baby; the clothes of a doll, like everything else in this world, get dirty – what will give more intense delight to a young girl than the washing and 'the getting up' of her dolls' linen? Is not all this life in miniature?

P.H. Chavasse, *Counsel to a Mother on the Care and Rearing of her Children*, 1874

BLEEDING AT THE NOSE

A nettle leaf put upon the tongue, and then pressed against the roof of the mouth, is sometimes efficacious in stopping bleeding at the nose; or a large key placed against the naked back.

The Modern Family Receipt Book, 1831

CLEANLINESS

The nurse should keep the child as clean as possible, and particularly she should train it to habits of cleanliness, so that it should feel uncomfortable when otherwise; watching especially that it does not soil itself in eating. At the same time, vanity in its personal appearance is not to be encouraged by overcare in this respect, or by too tight lacing or buttoning of dresses, nor a small foot cultivated by the use of tight shoes.

Mrs Isabella Beeton, *The Book of Household Management*, 1869

CARRYING AN INFANT

There is considerable art in carrying an infant comfortably for itself and for the nursemaid. If she carry it always seated upright on her arm, and presses it too closely against her chest, the stomach of the child is apt to get compressed, and the back fatigued. For her own comfort, a good nurse will frequently vary this position, by changing from one arm to the other, and sometimes by laying it across both, raising the head a little. When teaching it to walk, and guiding it by the hand, she should change the hand from time to time, so as to avoid raising one shoulder higher than the other. This is the only way in which a child should be taught to walk; leading-strings and other foolish inventions, which force an infant to make efforts, with its shoulders and head forward, before it knows how to use its limbs, will only render it feeble, and retard its progress.

Mrs Isabella Beeton, *The Book of Household Management*, 1869

GRUEL

Put two tablespoonfuls of oatmeal or prepared groats into a stewpan, and by degrees add a pint of water, mixing smoothly with a wooden spoon; place it upon the fire, keeping it well stirred, until it has boiled a couple of minutes, then pour it into a basin, add half a slat-spoonful of salt, two teaspoonfuls of brown sugar, and two ounces of butter, the latter especially; if for a cold in the chest even more than the quantity, should the stomach be strong enough to bear it.

Gruel when properly made, ought to adhere rather thickly to the back of the spoon, but not to be pastry; it ought likewise to be eaten directly it is made, or it becomes thick and unpleasant to eat; if required plain, omit all the seasoning; it might also be made with milk.

Alexis Soyer, *The Modern Housewife*, 1851

BRUISES

When the contusion is slight, fomentations of warm vinegar and water, frequently applied, will generally relieve it. Cataplasms of fresh cow-dung applied to bruises occasioned by violent blows or falls will seldom fail to have a good effect. Nothing however is more certainly efficacious than a porter plaster immediately applied to the part affected. Boil some porter in an earthen vessel over a slow fire till it is well thickened; and when cold, spread it on a piece of leather to form the intended plaster.

The Housekeeper's Receipt Book, 1813

RING WORMS

This eruption, which generally appears on the head in a circular form, attended with painful itching, is sometimes removed by rubbing it with black ink, or mushroom catchup. The following preparation is also recommended. Wash some roots of sorrel quite clean, bruise them in a mortar, and steep them in white vinegar for two or three days: then rub the liquor on the ring worm three or four times a day till it begin to disappear,

The Housekeeper's Receipt Book, 1813

HABITS AND PUNISHMENTS

Most children have some bad habit, of which they must be broken; but this is never accomplished by harshness without developing worse evils: kindness, perseverance, and patience in the nurse, are here of the utmost importance. When finger-sucking is one of these habits, the fingers are sometimes rubbed with bitter aloes, or some equally disagreeable substance. Others have dirty habits, which are only to be changed by patience, perseverance, and, above all, by regularity in the nurse. She should never be permitted to inflict punishment on these occasions, or, indeed, on any occasion. But, if punishment is to be avoided, it is still more necessary that all kinds of indulgence and flattery be equally forbidden. Yielding to all the whims of a child – picking up its toys when thrown away in mere wantonness, would be intolerable. A child should never be led to think others inferior to it, to beat a dog, or even the stone against which it falls, as some children are taught to do by silly nurses. Neither should the nurse affect or show alarm at any of the little accidents which must inevitably happen; if it falls, treat it as a trifle; otherwise she encourages a spirit of cowardice and timidity. But she will take care that such accidents are not of frequent occurrence, or the result of neglect.

Mrs Isabella Beeton, *The Book of Household Management*, 1869

SPRING APERIENTS

For children nothing is better than:– 1. Brimstone and treacle; to each tea-cupful of this, when mixed, add a tea-spoonful of cream of tartar. As this sometimes produces sickness, the following may be used:– 2. Take tartrate of soda one drachm and a half, powdered jalap and powdered rhubarb each fifteen grains, ginger two grains.

Mix: Dose for a child above five years, one small teaspoonful; above ten years, a large teaspoonful; above fifteen, half the whole, or two tea-spoonfuls; and a person above twenty, three tea-spoonfuls, or the whole, as may be required by the habit of the person. This medicine may be dissolved in warm water, common or mint tea. This powder can be kept for use in a wide-mouthed bottle, and be in readiness for any emergency. The druggist may be requested to treble or quadruple the quantities as convenient.

The Housekeeper, 1876

TO DESTROY VERMIN IN CHILDREN'S HEADS

Take one ounce of vinegar, one ounce of stavesacre, well powdered, half an ounce of honey, half an ounce of sulphur, and two ounces of sweet oil; mix the whole together into a liniment, and rub the head repeatedly with a little thereof. If the heads of children are well washed once a week with soap and water, they will be free from vermin.

The School of Arts; or, Fountain of Knowledge

FOR A COLD

Take a tea-cupful of linseed, a quarter of a pound of stick liquorice sliced, and a quarter of a pound of sun raisins, put them in two quarts of soft water, and let it simmer over a slow fire, till nearly reduced to one quart; then strain off, and add to it, while it is hot, a quarter of a pound of brown sugar-candy pounded.

James W. Laughton, *The General Receipt-Book*, c. 1845

DENTITION

When children are about cutting their teeth, they slaver much, are feverish, hot, and uneasy; their gums swell, and are very painful; they are sometimes loose in the bowels. and at other times costive; and occasionally convulsions come on.

Leeches are often serviceable when applied behind the ears; as are also blisters.

Samuel and Sarah Adams, *The Complete Servant*, 1825

SYRUP OF VOILETS

Take of fresh flowers of the violet, 1 lb. boiling distilled water, 3 pints. Macerate for 25 hours, and strain the liquor through a cloth, without pressing, and add double-refined sugar, to make the syrup.

This is an agreeable *laxative medicine* for young children

Samuel and Sarah Adams, *The Complete Servant*, 1825

CHINCOUGH OR HOOPING-COUGH

This disorder generally attacks children, to whom it often proves fatal for want of proper management. Those who breathe an impure air, live upon poor sustenance, drink much warm tea, and do not enjoy sufficient exercise are most subject to the convulsive cough. In the beginning of the disorder, the child should be removed to a change of air, and the juice of onions and horse-radish applied to the sole of the feet. The diet light and nourishing, and taken in small quantities; the drink must be lukewarm, consisting chiefly of toast and water, mixed with a little white wine. If the cough be attended with feverish symptoms, a gentle emetic must be taken of camomile flowers, and afterwards the following liniment applied to the pit of the stomach. Dissolve one scruple of tartar emetic in two ounces of spring water, and add half an ounce of the tincture of cantharides; rub a tea spoonful of it every hour on the lower region of the stomach with a warm piece of flannel, and let the wetted part be kept warm with the flannel. This will be found to be the best remedy for the hooping-cough.

The Housekeeper's Receipt Book, 1813

WORMS

Worms in children are denoted by paleness of the face, itching of the nose, grinding of the teeth during sleep, offensive breath, and nausea; the belly is hard and painful, and in the morning there is a copious flow of saliva, and an uncommon craving for dry food. Amongst a variety of other medicines for destroying worms in the human body, the following will be found effectual.– Make a solution of tartarized antimony, two grains in four ounces of water, and take two or three tea-spoonfuls three times a day for four days; and on the day following a purging powder of calomel and jalap, from three to six grains each. Or take half a pound of senna leaves well bruised, and twelve ounces of olive oil, and digest them together in a sand heat for four or five days.– Strain off the liquor, take a spoonful in the morning fasting, persevere in it, and it will be found effectual in the most obstinate cases.

The Housekeeper's Receipt Book, 1813

CUTTING OF TEETH

Great care is required in feeding young children during the time of cutting their teeth, as they often cry as if disgusted with food, when it is chiefly owing to the pain occasioned by the edge of a silver or metal spoon pressing on their tender gums. The spoon ought to be of ivory, bone, or wood, with the edges round and smooth, and care must be taken to keep it sweet and clean.

At this period, a moderate looseness, or a copious flow of saliva are favourable symptoms: with a view to promote the latter, the child should be suffered to gnaw such substances as tend to mollify the gums, and by their pressure to facilitate the protrusions. For this purpose, a piece of liquorice or marshmallow root will be of service; or the gums may be softened and relaxed by rubbing them with honey or sweet oil.

The Housekeeper's Receipt Book, 1813

Bibliography

A. F., *The Ladies' Pocket Book of Etiquette*, 1838

Acton, Eliza, *Modern Cookery for Private Families*, 1856

Adams, Samuel and Sarah, *The Complete Servant*, 1825

Balston, Thomas (ed.), *The Housekeeping Book of Susanna Whatman, 1776-1800*, 1956

Beeton, Mrs Isabella, *The Book of Household Management*, 1861, 1869 and 1888

Burnett, John (ed.), *Useful Toil. Autobiographies of Working People from the 1820s to the 1920s*, 1974

Censor, *Dont: A Manual of Mistakes and Improprieties more or less prevalent in Conduct and Speech*

Chavasse, P. H., *Counsel to a Mother on the Care and Rearing of her Children*, 1874

Clair, Colin, *Kitchen and Table*, 1964

Cobbett, Anne, *The English Housekeeper*, 1842

Consett, Thomas, *The Footman's Directory*, 1825

Copley, Esther, *Cottage Cookery*, 1849

Cunnington Phillis, *Costume of Household Servants from the Middle Ages to 1900*, 1974

Davies, N. E., *Nursery Hints*, 1884

Dawes, Frank, *Not in Front of the Servants*, 1973

Domestic Life

The Duties of a Lady's Maid, 1825

Duties of the Butler, 1858

Eland, G (ed.), *Purefoy Letters, 1735–53*, 1931

Faunthorpe, Rev J. P. (ed.), *Household Science: Readings in Necessary Knowledge for Girls and Young Women*, 1881

A Few Hints to Nursemaids, 1890

Fowler, John, and Cornforth, John, *English Decoration in the 18th Century*, 1974

Francatelli, C. E., *The Cook's Guide and Housekeeper's and Butler's Assistant*, 1877

Gathorne-Hardy, Jonathan. *The Rise and Fall of the British Nanny*, 1972

Gibbs, Mary Ann, *The Years of the Nannies*, 1960

Giles, Edward B., Mogford, John, Prewett, Frederick T., and Roberts,

Henry B., *The West-End Hand Book of British Liveries*

Girouard, Mark, *Life in the English Country House*, 1978

The Good Nurse, 1828

Greville, Lady Violet, 'Men-servants in England' in *National Review*, February 1892

Haan, David de, *Antique Household Gadgets and Appliances, c. 1860-*

1930, 1977

Harland, Marion, *Common Sense in the Nursery*, 1887

Harrison, Molly, *The Kitchen in History*, 1972

Horn, Pamela, *The Rise and Fall of the Victorian Servant*, 1975

The Household Cyclopaedia, 1856

The Housekeeper

The Housekeeper's Receipt Book, 1813

The Housewife's Receipt-Book, 1837

James, Philip (ed.), *A Butler's Recipe Book, 1719*, 1935

King-Hall, Magdalen, *The Story of the Nursery*, 1958

The Lady

Laughton, James W., *The General Receipt-Book*, c. 1845

Loudon, Mrs, *The Lady's Country Companion*, 1845

Marsh, J. J., *Nursery Handbook*, 1891

Marshall, Dr Dorothy, *The English Domestic Servants in History*, 1949

Marshall, Jo, *Kitchenware*, 1976

The Modern Family Receipt Book, 1831

A New System of Domestic Cookery, 1860 (first edition 1808)

A New System of Practical Domestic Economy, 1824

Ray, Elizabeth (ed.), *The Best of Eliza Acton*, 1968

Reynolds, M. E., *The Complete Art of Cookery*, 1848

Salis, Mrs de, *Wrinkles and Notions for Every Household*, 1890

The School of Arts; or Fountain of Knowledge

The Servants' Guide and Family Manual, 1830

Servants' Magazine

The Servants' Own Paper

The Servants' Practical Guide, 1880

Smith, Mrs, *The Female Economist*, 1810

Soyer, Alexis, *The Gastronomic Regenerator*, 1846

Soyer, Alexis, *The Modern Housewife*, 1851

Stuart, D. M., *The English Abigail*, 1946

Tannahill, Reay, *Food in History*, 1973

Things a Woman Wants to Know

The Times

Tschumi, Gabriel, *Royal Chef*, 1954

Turner, E. S., *What the Butler Saw*, 1962

Williams, James, *The Footman's Guide*

Wise, Dorothy (ed.), *Diary of William Tayler, Footman, 1837*, 1962

Glossary

Alembic — gourd-shaped vessel used in distilling

Alkanet — red dye obtained from the root of the Alkanet plant

Ambergris — wax-like substance found in tropical seas and in the intestines of sperm whales

Aqua vitae (acque vitae) — unrectified alcohol

Attar of Rose — fragrant essence derived from rose petals

Balm of Gilead — gold-coloured resin obtained from the tree *Balsamodendron Gileadense*

Bath brick — calcareous earth moulded into a brick

Bay salt — salt in large crystals obtained by evaporation, generally from sea water

Benjamin — benzoin, a resinous substance obtained from the tree *Styrax benzoin*

Black Lead — graphite

Bran — corn husks separated from the flour after grinding

Brazil — red dye derived from brazil-wood

Brimstone — sulphur

Calamus aromaticus — eastern aromatic plant, generally descriptive of the sweet-scented Lemon Grass of Malabar

Calomel — mercurous chloride

Carmine — red pigment obtained from cochineal

Castile (Castille) soap — hard, white or mottled soap made from olive oil and soda

Cataplasm — poultice

Caudle — warm, sweetened and spiced drink containing wine or ale given to invalids and their visitors

Cinchona bark — bark of the Peruvian tree or shrub cinchona

Civet — substance secreted by the civet cat with a strong musky smell

Clove-gillyflower — clove-scented pink

Compôte — fruit preserved in syrup

Cordial — sweet, fragrant beverage

Corrosive sublimate — mercuric chloride

Crocus martis — crocus of iron, a yellow or red powder obtained from metals by calcination

Cypress powder — powder from the aromatic root of the Sweet Cypress plant

Drachm — $^1/_8$ oz. (3.6 grams) Apothecaries' weight; $^1/_{16}$ oz. (1.8 grams) Avoirdupois

Dragon's blood — red gum from the fruit of the palm *Calamus Draco*

Dram — see Drachm

Emery — coarse corundum

Fine, to — to clarify or refine

Flitch — side (of bacon)

Fuller's earth — hydrous silicate of alumina

Gum ammoniac — gum of Ammon, resin obtained from the plant *Dorema Ammoniacum*

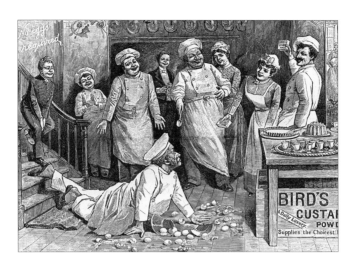

Gum mastic — resin obtained from the evergreen shrub *Pistacia Lentiscus*

Gum sandarac (sandrach) — resin obtained from the African tree *Callitris Quadrivalvis*

Gum shellac — dark-red resin obtained from certain trees when punctured by the cochineal insect

Hartshorn — hart's antlers, which, ground or flaked, were once the principal source of ammonia

Hogshead — large cask

Isinglass — semi-transparent gelatin for making jellies and clarifying liquors obtained from animals' hides and hoofs

Jalap — resin obtained from the roots of the Mexican climbing plant *Exogonium Purga*

Lamp black — soot from an oil or gas lamp

Laudanum — alcoholic tincture of opium

Lees — sediment from wine and other liquids

List — material made from the selvages of cloth

Loaf sugar — hard, refined sugar moulded into the shape of a cone

Lye — alkaline solution, water impregnated with alkaline salts obtained from vegetable ashes

Maiden vine — vine grown from a seed

Marshmallow — shrubby herb that grows near salt marshes with a soft root

Minim — drop, equivalent to $^1/_{60}$ fluid drachm

Muriatic acid — hydrochloric acid

Musk — substance secreted by the male musk-deer used as a basis of perfumes

Opodeldoc — soap liniment, solution of soap in alcohol with camphor and oils of origanum and rosemary

Oil of Florence — superior olive oil

Oil of rhodium — oil derived from rosewood

Oil of turpentine — volatile oil distilled

from the fluid obtained from coniferous trees

Oil of vitriol — concentrated sulphuric acid

Oil varnish — oil boiled to the consistency of varnish

Orris root — root of species of iris

Ottar — see Attar

Otto — see Attar

Pearl ash — potassium carbonate

Pipeclay — fine white clay used to make tobacco pipes

Pomade — scented ointment applied to the skin

Pomatum — see Pomade

Porter — porter's ale, dark beer with a bitter taste brewed partially charred malt

Pricked — sour or tainted

Race ginger — root of ginger

Ratafia — liqueur or cordial flavoured with peach, apricot or cherry kernels or almonds

Red lead — red oxide of lead

Rosin — solid residue obtained after the distillation of oil of turpentine from crude turpentine

Rottenstone — decomposed limestone

Salamander — circular iron plate with a handle

Sal-ammoniac — ammonium chloride

Salt of tartar — potassium carbonate

Silver litharge — lead, as a by-product in the separation of silver from lead

Size — glutinous wash used to bind pigments or as a ground for writing, painting or gilding

Snuffers — instrument used to snuff, or remove the unburnt wick from, a candle

Soft soap — semi-liquid soap made with potash lye

Spermaceti — fatty substances derived from the sperm whale

Spirit of turpentine — see Oil of turpentine

Spirit of wine — alcohol, rectified spirit

Stavesacre — seeds of the species *Delphinium Staphisagria*

Stomachic — potion good for the stomach

Stone blue — indigo mix with starch or whiting

Storax — resin derived from the storax-tree

Sugar candy — clarified crystallized sugar

Sugar of lead — lead acetate

Sweet oil — olive oil

Tincture of calumba — essence made with the root of the calumba tree

Tincture of cantharides — essence made with the dried beetle *Exogonium Purga*

Triturate, to — to reduce to a fine powder

Verdigris — acetate of copper, green deposit which forms naturally on copper and brass

White lead — compound of lead carbonate and hydrated oxide of lead

White vitriol — sulphate of zinc

Whiting (whitening) — powdered chalk

Yellow saunders (sanders) — sandalwood from the species *Santalum Freycinetianum*